THE ENERGY NATURE OF HUMAN EMOTIONS AND SEXUAL ATTRACTION

BOOKS BY PETER FRITZ WALTER

CREATIVE-C LEARNING: THE INNOVATIVE KINDERGARTEN

TAO TE CHING (ENGLISH AND GERMAN TRANSLATIONS)

DAS DAO DER STAATSFÜHRUNG UND STRATEGIE (GERMAN)

ÉCRITS POÉTIQUES (FRENCH)

ESSAYS ON LAW, POLICY, AND PSYCHIATRY (14 VOLUMES)

EVIDENCE AND BURDEN OF PROOF IN SOVEREIGN IMMUNITY LITIGATION: A PROCEDURAL GUIDE FOR INTERNATIONAL LAWYERS AND GOVERNMENT COUNSEL (DOCTORAL THESIS)

GREAT MINDS SERIES (11 VOLUMES)

INTEGRATE YOUR EMOTIONS: A GUIDE TO EMOTIONAL WHOLENESS

LITIGATION PRACTICE AND BURDEN OF PROOF UNDER THE FOREIGN SOVEREIGN IMMUNITIES ACT, 1976: A PROCEDURAL GUIDE FOR INTERNATIONAL LAWYERS IN THE UNITED STATES AND CANADA

POETIC WRITINGS 1990-2010 (STORIES, PAMPHLETS, POEMS, ESSAYS)

POETISCHE SCHRIFTEN (GERMAN)

SCHOLARLY ARTICLES (21 VOLUMES)

SHAMANIC WISDOM MEETS THE WESTERN MIND

THE 12 ANGULAR POINTS OF SOCIAL JUSTICE AND PEACE

THE BETTER LIFE: TRANSFORMING YOURSELF FROM INSIDE OUT

THE ENERGY NATURE OF HUMAN EMOTIONS AND SEXUAL ATTRACTION: A SYSTEMIC ANALYSIS OF EMOTIONAL IDENTITY IN THE PROCESS OF THE HUMAN SEXUAL RESPONSE

THE LEADERSHIP I CHING: YOUR DAILY COMPANION FOR PRACTICAL GUIDANCE

THE NEW PARADIGM SERIES (BOOK REVIEWS, 3 VOLUMES)

THE VIBRANT NATURE OF LIFE: A SCIENCE-BASED PATHWAY FOR A BETTER, RICHER, AND MORE ABUNDANT LIFE

WALTER'S CAREER AND LEADERSHIP SERIES (3 VOLUMES)

THE ENERGY NATURE OF HUMAN EMOTIONS AND SEXUAL ATTRACTION

A Systemic Analysis of Emotional Identity in the Process of the Human Sexual Response

by Peter Fritz Walter

About the Author

Parallel to an international law career in Germany, Switzerland and the United States, Dr. Peter Fritz Walter (Pierre) focused upon fine art, cookery, astrology, musical performance, social sciences and humanities.

He started writing essays as an adolescent and received a high school award for creative writing and editorial work for the school magazine.

After finalizing his law diplomas, he graduated with an LL.M. in European Integration at Saarland University, Germany, in 1982, and with a Doctor of Law title from University of Geneva, Switzerland, in 1987.

He then took courses in psychology at the University of Geneva and interviewed a number of psychotherapists in Lausanne and Geneva, Switzerland. His interest was intensified through a hypnotherapy with an Ericksonian American hypnotherapist in Lausanne. This led him to the recovery and healing of his inner child.

After a second career as a corporate trainer and personal coach, Pierre retired in 2004 as a full-time writer, philosopher and consultant.

His nonfiction books emphasize a systemic, holistic, cross-cultural and interdisciplinary perspective, while his fiction works and short stories focus upon education, philosophy, perennial wisdom, and the poetic formulation of an integrative worldview.

Pierre is a German-French bilingual native speaker and writes English as his 4th language after German, Latin and French. He also reads source literature for his research works in Spanish, Italian, Portuguese, and Dutch. In addition, Pierre has notions of Thai, Khmer, Chinese, Japanese, and Vietnamese.

Dedicated to the Wilhelm Reich (1897-1957), the first sex researcher who discovered the missing link between the human sexual function and the energy nature of human emotions.

The author's profits from this book are being donated to charity.

CONTENTS

PREFACE

Glimpses of a New Science

✳

In the present book I am going to propose a vocabulary I have created do elucidate a perennial science I discovered to be existing since times of old and that could be called 'The Science of the Bioenergy.'

Why do we need vocabularies?

I admit that it's a bit odd to ask such a commonplace question, but when you see how many misunderstandings even in high-quality science publications are created by the mere fact that people use words in different ways, you want to be to the point when you say A is A and B is B.

Now, different researchers have discovered basically the same things, but they gave them

different names. Reichenbach spoke of the 'odic force' and Mesmer of 'animal magnetism.'

And different cultures again use different names. The Chinese speak of *ch'i*, the Japanese of *ki*, the Indians of *prana* and most of the native cultures of *mana* when they talk about what Reich called 'cosmic life energy' and which in modern scientific terms we would rather call the 'quantum field' or the 'cosmic energy field.'

How can we ever discuss this force, then, if we have to use a thousand names for it?

I try to put an end to this confusion and simply call this universal energy 'e-force,' and the ultimate creator principle that is at the basis of this force, I am going to call 'e.'

You may call it 'the ultimate observer,' God or Tao, but for scientific discussion and publication, I simply call it 'e.'

Now I go one step ahead and say I won't write about this huge subject in general but only about what this means for research on emotions and for answering the question what emotions truly are. And I found that there is indeed something like an

'emotional identity code' that, like an ID tag, every sentient being possesses and that individualizes us. And as a result of this discovery, I created *Emonics* which is a short form of 'Emotional Identity Code Science.'

What does this science do? It researches into and explicates the functionality of our emotions; to see that emotions are ultimately but flowing cosmic energy, and not, as our psychologists say, static elements of cognitive reasoning, means to predict far-reaching changes in our landscapes of psychology and sexology.

I will thus focus upon elucidating the nature of what sexologists call 'sexual drives' and what I call 'emotional predilections.' They speak of *sex* and I speak of *emotions*.

That is indeed a significant difference. The difference is more than significant, it is crucial. They more or less say that sex comes first and I say emotions come first. They say that sexual drives are self-executing automatisms. *Emonics* says that sexual desire follows emotional choice and predilection. We are in for a change here, and not a minor one.

To begin with, I argue that psychiatrists who affirm that abuse cannot be healed, thereby alleging that the *abused invariably become the abusers,* argue from a cave point of view, to speak with Plato. Within their reductionist and mechanical system, where life is cut down to a *residual concept,* they think they are arguing in truth. But they are sitting in a glasshouse. Most of the people who work in these professional areas are not knowledgeable, and do not need to be, about cutting-edge science. It's not up to them to change the system, and they'd anyway not do it. So the initiative has to come from our universities, and professional associations, and pass from there right to our parliaments and political leaders for changing what needs to be changed, and for reforming what needs to be reformed.

For triggering a discussion about how to look at human sexuality in the future, I have suggested a *unifying terminology,* to begin with. The terminology could namely facilitate cross-disciplinary exchanges between scientists, professionals, politicians and the public at large. To repeat it, I call this scientific terminology *Emonics (Emotional Identity Code Science),* an abbreviation that reflects the essential,

the fact that we all possess as individuals a *unique emotional identity, and identity code*, which is a vibrational fingerprint.

This means that we are not automatons in matters of emotions and sexuality, as early Freudian theory and later sexology believe. It means that we are emotionally aware individuals who can make conscious choices in all matters of emotional and sexual predilection.

It means that when we choose certain partners for sexual mating, this is not done from a compulsion, except in neurosis or psychosis, but from a point of view of *emotional predilection*. To speak specifically about *pedophilia* in this context, the main reason why adults relate to children sexually is that they relate *emotionally* to them in the first place, and *not* the other way around, that they relate sexually to them in the first place.

Thus, when researching about how to help men and women who suffer from the social despise that their attraction incurs in present society, we have to consider these persons reflecting about their emotional predilection for children, and reason it out, to render it fully conscious.

It is namely not conducive, for this purpose, to let them focus on the sexual part of their attraction as their sexual attraction is *a consequence of their emotional predilection* that for reasons we do not really know, *sexualized,* while in the case of most other people who feel emotionally closer to children than to adults, many teachers and child care workers, such sexualization of their *primal emotional predilection* does regularly not occur.

Thus for science the way to find the light in these complex matters, research has to focus not on the end result, the sexual attraction itself, but to what is prior to it, namely *why and how the initial emotional predilection for children turned sexual.*

This research has to my knowledge never been done, which is why we do not have conclusive results, which in turn gives right to those who say that abuse cannot be healed because pedophilia is as it were a condition that is, in their opinion, 'inborn and cannot be changed.' This latter conclusion is a typical Socratic error, because the conclusion was based upon a knowledge gap, and is thus, theoretically speaking, a *false conclusion.*

There may be certain factors, like childhood experiences or deep hurt and trauma experienced in childhood, that predispose certain people to relate more easily to children emotionally, or to feel safer with children than with adults. In this sense, pedophilia is a childhood hangup and thus has something pathological about it.

But this attraction to children who bond with one's inner child does not per se account for the sexualization of these emotional longings; to repeat it, many educators have the same emotional preference, which is why they became educators in the first place, without however experiencing sexual attraction for their emotional love objects. Theoretically speaking, it could well also be possible that all those educators do actually experience at least temporary sexual longings for the children of their predilection, but repress and deny those feelings, or simply hide them and never talk about them.

We cannot per se exclude this possibility, and it needs to be tackled scientifically, because if this is true or not is actually of paramount importance. If it's true, then emotional predilection would dispose a

person to be sexual with the objects of their emotional choice, without a 'sexualization' of such *pedoemotions* being necessary.

While I do not exclude this possibility, I found it more likely that per se, pedoemotions are *not sexualized* but need a special 'trigger' to become sexual, but I so far ignore what this trigger could be. So what I am doing, humbly so, is just to open the discussion along *certain rational lines* that are promising enough to allow us certain positive expectations for a new and better handling of sexual paraphilias in the future.

I do not know any definite answers, but sound research can well provide them, if for one time, it's conducted with scientific honesty, and without all those myths and fairy tales coming in that pervade presently the public debate to a point that the bulk of scientists cautiously keep away from being involved in it—and for good reason. There needs to be a certain form of backup, either from universities or from the political arena, or both, so that such research is considered respectable and noble enough for scientists to engage in it, namely without losing their scientific reputation.

I have equally demonstrated in other publications that the Western point of view is the exception when we compare it with the science traditions of most of our 200 countries around the world. Most of our cultures namely recognize the *energy nature of human emotions*, and thus could quite easily comprehend my social policy and research propositions, while for the strictly Western point of view, it's quite an outrageous and outlandish idea so far; else, it would be held 'esoteric' and relegated to 'new age literature,' which would probably render my quest illusionary that both mainstream *science and psychiatry* have to tackle these issues under a new light.

I also will show in this book that there is well an alternative science tradition established in all Western nations, with more or less convincing alternative research results, that argues along the lines of my theory, and which has prepared the scientific ground in our culture for a more thorough discussion and elaboration of a healing or treatment concept for sexual paraphilias, as a primary step for their social integration.

And we need to see and argue out, on a collective level, the reasons why we need this integration. Namely, as a lawyer I need to emphasize that only integration brings peace and peaceful togetherness, while it can be shown both through history science and cross-cultural and historical legal research that *disintegration always brought about chaos*, crime and projections, and thus scapegoat slaughtering, up to large-scale violence and genocide as a result.

Now, let me give you an overview over the new terminology I created and which I am going to use in this book.

Emonics is a science vocabulary I have created. The name is an abbreviation of *Emotional Identity Code Science*. Purpose of the vocabulary is to facilitate scientific investigation of human emotions as a vibrational phenomenon, and research on the human energy field.

Research on emotions that I conducted over more than twenty years has given me conclusive evidence that every human being possesses a unique emotional identity code, something like a vibrational ID number, that works like a cosmic identifier and sets us apart as absolutely unique beings. This is valid not

only for humans but this vibrational pattern is unique also for animals, for plants and even for inanimate matter such as rocks.

Emonics research discovered in human emotions a quality that traditional research on emotions overlooked. While traditional psychology has to some extent admitted the cognitive nature of emotions, it has related emotions to thought and perception only and located them in the brain. Emonics, in accordance with a number of perennial science traditions, clairvoyant science, and cutting-edge research on the human energy field shows that emotions are located in the human aura or luminous energy field, and that they possess an inherent quality of *flow*.

Emonics research shows that thought and emotions are vibrational patterns that flow through our etheric or luminous body. In this sense, also animals and plants do have emotions, simply because they also partake in the cosmic energy field. Hence, Emonics research can be said to transcend psychology and to some extent unify biology, psychology, parapsychology and physics into something like a *unified field theory of emotions* that

holistically inquires into the nature of emotional identity.

I call 'e' the creator identity, which is the functional complement of consciousness.

Consciousness is a function of e in that e and consciousness are a functional whole.

E manifests on this planet as *e-force*. Shifts in consciousness bring about shifts in e-force, which in turn trigger altered states of consciousness. Superconsciousness is a state of e-force at its peak level.

Disintegration of emotions occurs through repression and denial. The results are violence, regression and sadism—which are obstacles to evolution.

The biogenic positive charge accumulated in living organisms leads, typically, to discharge in the form of ecstatic convulsions or sexual orgasm and is part of the inherent self-regulatory system of the cell plasma.

The conscious perception of our *emonic flow* includes the lucid awareness of our emotional predilection and sexual attraction in every given

moment or situation. For example, nurses should be conscious of their organism's emonic flow regarding patients they are working with; educators need to develop emonic awareness in order to prevent falling in the trap of sexual codependence and abuse.

The bioenergetic current flows through the organism, from the cell plasma to the periphery and into the luminous body and again back from the luminous body to the cell, depending on the polarity of the current. When it is positive, it is expansive and flows from the cell to the periphery (joy); when it is negative, it retreats from the periphery back into the cell (fear). Emonic flow, in popular language, may be expressed as *emotional flow*, and I do indeed use both terms synonymously.

These flow principles inherent in the nature of the bioenergy are also at work, negatively, in the etiology of sadism. In the natural sexual streaming of the bioenergy, that Wilhelm Reich described as 'hot, melting streaming,' the energy during orgasm explodes from the cell toward the luminous body.

In sadism, however, because of the muscular armor in the pelvis region and other parts of the body, the energy cannot freely flow outwardly and therefore

is repelled back with the result that instead of relaxing joy and expansive feelings, what is felt after orgasm is depression, anxiety, and fatigue. These latter symptoms then, can also be used as signals in diagnosing sadism. As a result of these insights, it is possible to actually heal sadism by getting the emonic current again to flow naturally through the entire organism.

This can be done through muscular *relaxation* or through consciousness work, using a self-coaching technique which I created and termed 'Life Authoring,' or else a combination of these with methods practiced by alternative Medicine, such as body work, massage, *Qigong*, *Tai Chi Chuan*, *Reiki*, or *Yoga*.

Children and babies naturally, when they are swinging in their continuum balance, are within the realm of emonic integrity.

Emonic sanity is manifest when emotional energy is integrated, which is the natural condition in the living organism. This can also be called *emotional balance*. Emonic sanity if further characterized by high complexity and high emotional and erotic intelligence. Integration occurs ideally on three levels:

▸ Multisensorial (Spirituality)

▸ Extrasensorial (Parapsychology)

▸ Sensorial (Eroticism, Sexuality)

Emonic sanity with children is a task of every parent and every educator; the task consists in caring for preserving the natural continuum balance of the child.

This means in practice to observe a principle of *sacred non-interference* in the child's body or mind continuum, to restrain from inflicting educational violence on the child, to respect the child's privacy, to actively care to awaken and develop the child's unique gifts and talents, to allow the child their own social life, which means to abstain from rigidly controlling the child's friendships, to give the child real opportunities for an early art career if the child is gifted, to restrain from emotional manipulation of the child, and to help the child accept their body and emotions through loving dialogue about all life situations, without taboo.

Emonic setup means our natural bioenergetic setup from birth, the free flow of the vital energies in

our organism, the healthy vibration of the protoplasm, the natural cycle of charge and discharge in our sexual embrace, during the whole of the life cycle from conception to death.

Our emonic setup is by nature harmonious and self-regulated, and it favors equitable relationships, love and natural sharing of emotions, joy, and goodness. It becomes distorted through early interference with the natural energy pattern in form of educational violence, emotional manipulation and abuse, and the obstruction of the emonic flow through the educational moralistic prohibition of expressing emotions and sexual wishes through truthful dialogue.

Emonic vibration is the bioenergetic flow and unique vibrational code that is inherent in every living organism, and without which life would cease and death would occur. Emonic vibration is thus an immediate characteristic of life.

INTRODUCTION

A New Regard Upon the Human Sexual Function

✳

Valerie Hunt relates a mind-boggling story in her book *Infinite Mind, Science of the Human Vibrations of Consciousness (2000)*; the anecdote Hunt relates can be used as a metaphor for introducing a daringly new regard on sexual paraphilias:

> In Kyoto, Japan, at the famous Pain Control Clinic, I watched acupuncture and moxibustion treatments, the latter using a small herbal cone placed on acupuncture points and lighted like incense. With arthritis, moxibustion gave faster pain relief than our conventional therapeutic techniques.
>
> One day, an ambulance brought a woman to the pain clinic with second degree steam burns on both arms. She screamed with the pain. The common procedure in America was to first inject narcotics to ease the pain, followed by tissue cooling and ointment. Instead, the Pain Control Clinic therapists wrapped both arms in household aluminum foil, to which they

attached a clothespin clamp with a lead wire ending in an acupuncture needle. The needle was inserted into the acupuncture point just below the kneecap on the opposite leg. This constituted the entire treatment.

In a few minutes the burn victim quieted; her face relaxed. In 20 minutes she was totally free of pain. The swollen, turgid, red-blue tissue looked pink and near normal. After three or four more daily treatments, her skin was normal without ulceration, peeling, or scars. The attending physician explained that the steam had created cellular metabolic disturbances affecting the energy field, which caused energy from other areas of the body to rush to the arms to heal them. This excess energy pressed on nerves and blood vessels, causing swelling and pain.

He stated that the aluminum foil, wire, and acupuncture needles drained the excess energy from the burned arms back into the legs—a simple, yet profound, explanation.

— Valerie V. Hunt, Infinite Mind (2000), p. 17.

According to traditional Western medicine, acupuncture is *charlatanism* because the premise it is based upon is considered to be inexistent: the cosmic life energy is in the opinion of most medical doctors the fruit of paranoid delusions. According to Western ignorance in white coats, exact science has never proven the existence of the *ether* or of any creator

energy. With the same ignorant arrogance, Western psychiatry continues to emphasize that abuse 'cannot be healed.'

Many psychiatrists, and among them especially those who work in forensic research and for law enforcement, take it for granted that abuse will be perpetuated through the fact that the abused invariably become the abusers. As I oppose this negativistic, largely ignorant and cynical approach since years, I have been looking for new solutions that are little known to most psychiatrists because they have been developed mainly outside of the Western world and scientific framework.

Western psychiatry may well be right in that from their reductionist view of the psyche, they will be short of tools for healing the scars of early abuse, and this logically so within their system simply because they, with the rest of Western science and medicine, *negate the energy-nature of all life* in general, and of the human organism, in particular.

And here they represent truly a minority position compared to the overwhelming majority of cultures that explain life since millennia as a *manifestation of the cosmic energy,* and which have developed

energy-based healing approaches for healing the body and the psyche.

One of the most generally known of these wistful traditions is *Chinese Medicine*; besides, there are innumerable tribal cultures that developed long ago their own energy-based healing systems.

> —See Peter Fritz Walter, Alternative Medicine and Wellness Techniques (Scholarly Articles, Vol. 3), 2015.

And there is Huna, the age-old spiritual culture and religion of the *Kahunas* in Hawaii.

I will put a particular focus in this context on the research on Huna conducted over many years by Max Long and Erika Nau.

The luminous body is one of several terms used for the transparent energy emanation around our physical body that manifests as an egg-shaped aura of different density, but generally of lower density than our physical body. Other terms that I have found in the scientific and esoteric literature *are aura, energy body, transparent body, luminous body, light body, particle body, etheric body,* and *spherical body.* In addition to looking at newer research on healing

the luminous body and summarizing approaches to energy healing from the past that have been suppressed and demonized by the dominator forces of reductionist modern science, I am going to propose first of all a *vocabulary* created in an attempt to unify terminology and help psychology develop an energy-based concept for understanding human emotions and sexual attraction. I do not arrogate myself to be a science creator; it is obvious that what I am presenting here is but a vocabulary or terminology, and not a complete science.

What I do is *trying to unify a very split-up and nonsensical terminology* that has grown historically, but not systemically. What I try to do is to look at the bioenergy in a *systemic way*, using the frame of reference of a modern holistic science, and especially systems theory.

—See Fritjof Capra, The Systems View of Life: A Unifying Vision (2014).

Here, my focus is especially on emotions, and how they impact upon the upcoming of sexual longings.

This is the core of my research, and this is where and how I want to impact on current sexology. Up to a

new generation of scientists to take up my torso of research and develop it into a grown-out science that can possibly and hopefully one day replace the *joke-forum of sexology* with its jesters, its clowns, its ridiculous assumptions, its 'phallometric' tests, and all the rest of make-believe knowledge it professes to possess.

There will be a time when serious science authors will deplore the decades the world has slept in safe hypnosis and under the spell of such a treacherous accumulation of myths and fairy tales that today is sold as official sexological science.

It will one day be proven that 1960s-born sexology was one of the most Cartesian approaches ever to be found in modern science, and even in the whole of science history!

CHAPTER ONE

The Energy Nature of Sexual Attraction

＊

One of the most important scientific research targets is elucidating the true nature of *human sexuality* and what I call *emotional predilections*.

The perennial science I rediscovered was a true science because it never lost its original continuum of being a true *philos sophia*, a science that was inspired by the *love for truth*, for wisdom.

Western culture, however, stands out by its collective denial of the most fundamental patterns of living. In our scientific tradition, scientists who acknowledged the existence of the *bioplasmatic energy* were rejected, defamed and persecuted by their system conform colleagues, and even some of their books were burnt. And yet this denial of truth that seems to be inherent in Western civilization is not

existent elsewhere in human history and mythology, as Joseph Campbell affirms in his books.

—See Peter Fritz Walter, Joseph Campbell and the Lunar Bull (Great Minds Series, Vol. 7), 2015.

In fact, all other large civilizations have since millennia acknowledged the fact that life is basically a function of energy and that's dynamic and systemic, and not static and mechanical. And from this principle, that in the Hermetic tradition was metaphorically expressed with 'as it is above, so it is below,' it appears in line with functional logic that what is inside the cell will also be enveloping the body. In fact, this bioplasmatic energy is both inside the cell and it surrounds the physical body like a transparent shell. It folds seven subtle energy layers around the physical or dense body that extent more than just a few inches.

— See, for example, Shafica Karagulla, The Chakras (1989).

From their erudite energy-based worldview, traditional Chinese and Tibetan medicine as well as Ayurveda from India were able to discover in our

organism the *meridians* as the major pipelines of the bioenergetic flow, and could develop the tremendously effective *medical science of acupuncture.*

The successes this perennial medical science booked already thousands of years ago are to this day today unheard-of in our mechanistic, symptom-oriented, chemistry-based and palliative Western medicine.

Despite *quantum physics,* which shattered much of the traditional Cartesian and nature-hostile scientific worldview, Western science continues to deny what is obvious: that life is holistically coded in *energy patterns* and that no living process can be properly mapped and identified in its functional effectiveness without knowing these patterns and the bioenergy charge they contain.

Even avant-garde systems researchers such as Rupert Sheldrake deny what they call the 'vitalistic approach' declaring a scientific roof paradigm that integrates the perennial knowledge about the cosmic life energy, against all scientific logic, as *mechanistic.*

— Rupert Sheldrake, A New Science of Life (1995), pp. 12 and 43-49. In addition, Sheldrake says morphogenetic information is not related to energy patterns, without giving a valid explanation for his hypothesis.

Sheldrake denies 'vitalistic' theories, of which he does not seem to grasp the one single truth behind the many expressions of it, the status of a theory, as they lack, according to him falsifiability, or refutability, or testability.

And here we are left alone, after a cathedral judgment of far-reaching consequences, and which is not followed by any evidence or reference; and such an author is credited with being one of the leading scientists today.

With Ervin Laszlo, it is even worse: he never mentions in his famous and bestselling books any of the authors that I reference not only in the following paragraph, but throughout this book, to come up with an *Integral Theory of Everything* that says all what those authors said over the course of several centuries, but he says it under the header *A-Field*, a term that sounds suspiciously close to Harold Saxton Burr's *L-Field*. And without mentioning Burr with one

word! And what Heraclites, Paracelsus, Goethe, Mesmer, Swedenborg, Freud, Jung, Einstein, Reichenbach, Reich, Lakhovsky or Bohm had to say about it goes unnoticed. Such a sworn resistance against knowledge that is perennial is all-too-typical for the arrogant attitude of most Western scientists and their mouthpiece media.

I really think that Western science is misguided from the start in that it always had this tendency to discard from its scientific worldview much more than it ever observed and retained. Think only of *Feng Shui*, the *Druid* sages, the *fairy worlds, shamanism, plant energies, morphogenetic fields, ectoplasms, telepathy, telekinesis, prophecy, astrology, numerology,* or *channeling:* these branches, and many more, of the great tree of knowledge were cut off from the *rudimentary torso* of official Western science, while great minds and brains have spent lifetimes researching in these fundamental disciplines of perennial science.

—There are basically twelve, and probably more, characteristics of holistic science that are to be found in perennial science. These twelve emanations or branches of the tree of knowledge remain still forbidden to most

humans today because they follow the oversoul of the mass media, instead of following their own lucid inner voice. Ancient traditional cultures and their scientific traditions, and what we today call perennial philosophy were holistic; they embraced flow principles, and they were truly scientific, but not scientific in a sense of being reductionist. They looked at life as a Gestalt, and derived conclusions from the observation of the living and moving, not from the dead. Here are the twelve branches of the ancient tree of knowledge: 1) Science and Divination; 2) Science and Energy; 3) Science and Flow; 4) Science and Gestalt; 5) Science and Intent; 6) Science and Intuition; 7) Science and Knowledge; 8) Science and Pattern; 9) Science and Perception; 10) Science and Philosophy; 11) Science and Truth; 12) Science and Vibration.

Mechanists are unable to understand nature, and they can for this very reason not understand a science that contains more than intellectual assumptions. And more importantly, their *spiritual vacuum* makes for their discarding out the very energy that is at the basis of all we observe.

The overarching universal creator principle that in religions is attributed to the divine and was given many names, I call it simply *e*, and this simplicity should exactly reflect its ultimate complexity.

To more aptly describe the creator force or meta-observer of reality, which in the film *What the Bleep Do We Know!?* is called the *ultimate observer*, I have added-on a second term, *e-force*. While *e* could be described as the *unmanifest ultimate observer*, *e-force* is a state of manifestation of the creator force.

E-force, then, is the force, the energy, through which *e* is acting upon the surface of *consciousness*.

It is very important to realize that *e* and consciousness are one in the sense that *e* instantaneously impacts upon and forms consciousness, while it is in turn aware of *e*.

It can be said as well that *e* or *e-force* are contained in consciousness. Now, on the human level, *e-force* has created human emotions, and is contained in emotional energy.

Thus, emotional energy is one of the many manifestations of the *e-force*. Let me give an

example. I cite from *Life after Death (1975)*, by Neville Randall:

> Leslie Flint was said to have a strange and rare gift, the ability to attract the spirits of human beings who had died and moved on to another place of existence, and to provide them with a substance called ectoplasm which they drew from his and his sitters' bodies to fashion a replica of the vocal organs—a voice box or etheric microphone. Through this peculiar contraption located about three feet above the medium's head, Woods was told, a spirit transmitted his thoughts. By a process that no living scientist could explain, the disincarnate spirit created vibrations which enabled him to speak to us as using a telephone, in a voice like the one he had on earth.

Now, this phenomenon can well be scientifically explained. We are observing here what is called by the secret science of Huna a 'protruding aka finger,' a bioplasmatic substance squeezed out from the body's reservoir of *e-force*, that the Kahunas call *mana*. This substance acts like a matrix for energetically coded messages and decodes them so that they can be intelligible for people who live in dimensions vibrating at a different frequency from the emitter's. Through the use of *aka substance*, we can thus construe a translator and transmitter device to help people

communicate who live in different energetic universes.

That ectoplasm box is exactly such kind of a device. It not only decodes the emonic vibrations from the other dimension, but also amplifies them so that these vibrations become sound waves intelligible for the human ear.

Of course, conventional science cannot explain these phenomena so far, because it has no explanation for the cosmic energy field that is the information field behind all those phenomena. It has built a neat house without giving the owner a room for himself. The owner of the house, that I call *e*, is the creator force. Western science truly is death science as it refuses to acknowledge the main ingredient of life, the *field* or life energy.

Why this is so has historical reasons. After more than a millennium of life and knowledge denial by the Christian Church, the mechanist scientists built a science that was to oppose the church, that had to be a science where God was banned.

Amit Goswami observes in his book *The Self-Aware Universe (1995)* that the major weakness of

material realism was 'that the philosophy seems to exclude subjective phenomena altogether.'

Do we have to wonder, then, that modern science until this day could not inquire into the nature of emotions without facing an abyss? This can't be different after all since modern science has no idea of the impact of the observer until the severe paradoxes of quantum physics blew up most of Newtonian science and healed that scientific neurosis, in order to reinstate nature, and e, in the house of natural science.

I would have to cite quite a few modern-day authors, if this was a study about the bioenergy in general, and not only in its impact on, and expression through, human emotions.

There is definitely a holistic trend now in postmodern science, and a new direction toward integration; and accordingly, there is a marked change of direction now in Western science that is gradually getting us again in touch with the spiritual dimension that has been discarded out; and from here we are going to gradually formulate, probably through a joint effort of many enlightened and spiritually aware scientists a *unified field theory*, or the

recognition of *The Field*, as Lynne McTaggart calls the life force in her book with the same title.

CARL-GUSTAV JUNG (1875-1961)

Carl Jung puts up an astonishing analogy between the Platonic concept of ideas, and the concept of energy in his study *Archetypes of the Collective Unconscious*, saying that at bottom there is no difference between Plato's *eîdos* concept and Jung's proprietary concept of *psychic energy* that he considered to be a constituent element in archetypes.

—Carl-Gustav Jung, Archetypes of the Collective Unconscious (1959), p. 639.

By the way, Jung honestly admits that the term *archetypes*, contrary to common belief, is not his invention, but to be found already with Cicero, Pliny, and others and that it also appears in the *Corpus Hermeticum* as a philosophical concept.

Looking at the old Greek term for archetype, *to archetypon eîdos*, it becomes clear that an archetype is just one possible form of eîdos.

— Id., p. 639, note 14.

Thus, Jung's insight about ideas containing energy as archetypes contain psychic energy, is sound and consequent. The *eîdos*, Jung explains, are primordial images stored in a supracelestial place as eternal, transcendent forms that the seer could perceive in dreams and visions. From this point of departure, Jung pursues:

> Or let us take the concept of energy, which is an interpretation of physical events. In earlier times it was the secret fire of the alchemists, or phlogiston, or the heat-force inherent in matter, like the primal warmth of the Stoics, or the Heraclitean ever-living fire, which border on the primitive notion of an all-pervading vital force, a power of growth and magic healing that is generally called mana. (Id., 397)

We are going to see further down that Jung, as if in a flash of genius, got a glimpse in what today the quantum physicist Fritjof Capra calls the *Web of Life* in his 1997 book with the same title.

In a couple of sentences Jung draws a synchronistic ellipse from Heraclites over the alchemists to today's still existing tribal cultures that call the universal cosmic energy *mana*.

Jung's insights are the most substantial, as he carefully analyses the nature of what he termed psychic energy, and distinguishes it from Freud's *libido* concept and the energy concept in atomic physics. In *On The Nature of the Psyche (1959)*, Jung writes:

> There are indications that psychic processes stand in some sort of energy relation to the physiological substrate. In so far as they are objective events, they can hardly be interpreted as anything but energy processes, or to put it another way: in spite of the non-measurability of psychic processes, the perceptible changes effected by the psyche cannot possibly be understood except as a phenomenon of energy. This places the psychologist in a situation which is highly repugnant to the physicist: The psychologist also talks of energy although he has nothing measurable to manipulate, besides which the concept of energy is a strictly defined mathematical quantity which cannot be applied as such to anything psychic. The formula for kinetic energy, $E=mv2/2$, contains the factors m (mass) and v (velocity), and these would appear to be incommensurable with the nature of the empirical psyche. If psychology nevertheless insists on employing its own concept of energy for the purpose of expressing the activity (energeia) of the psyche, it is not of course being used as a mathematical formula, but only

as its analogy. But note: this analogy is itself an older intuitive idea from which the concept of physical energy originally developed. The latter rests on earlier applications of an energeia not mathematically defined, which can be traced back to the primitive or archaic idea of the 'extraordinarily potent'. This mana concept is not confined to Melanesia, but can also be found in Indonesia and on the east coast of Africa; and it still echoes in the Latin numen and, more faintly, in genius (e.g., genius loci). The use of the term libido in the newer medical psychology has surprising affinities with the primitive mana. This archetypal idea is therefore far from being only primitive, but differs from the physicist's conception of energy by the fact that it is essentially qualitative and not quantitative.

—Carl-Gustav Jung, On the Nature of the Psyche (1959), pp. 130-132.

While I question Jung in several points, it is highly interesting, that, as only very few Western psychologists, he has been aware of the *perennial concept of a universal all-pervasive cosmic energy* that, in accordance with most tribal cultures, he calls *mana*. He never went as far as actually considering this energy as a *real and measurable information field* and not just an archetypal idea, but he well lays out

the conceptual problem that is at the basis of all present research on the cosmic life energy.

What Jung further explains regarding the difference between psychic energy and kinetic energy does not stand a deeper analysis. I am going to show further down that there is *no basic difference* between psychic energy and kinetic energy, but that their apparent difference only stems from the fact that they are measured in different ways.

Jung, rather closed to this idea, states that psychic energy could *not be measured or quantified*, other than by feeling :

> In psychology the exact measurement of quantities is replaced by an approximate determination of intensities, for which purpose, in strictest contrast to physics, we enlist the function of feeling (valuation). The latter takes the place, in psychology, of concrete measurement in physics. The psychic intensities and their graduated differences point to quantitative processes which are inaccessible to direct observation and measurement. While psychological data are essentially qualitative, they also have a sort of latent physical energy, since psychic phenomena exhibit a certain qualitative aspect. Could these quantities be measured the psyche would be bound to appear as having motion in space, something

to which the energy formula would be applicable. Therefore, since mass and energy are of the same nature, mass and velocity would be adequate concepts for characterizing the psyche so far as it has any observable effects in space: in other words, it must have an aspect under which it would appear as mass in motion. (Id., 132)

It appears to me Jung wanted to anticipate possible criticism from the side of his opponents, those who, following a mechanistic paradigm in psychology, would deny the idea of psychic energy as being a true dynamic force. And for justifying the energy nature of the psyche, he makes an awkward comparison with physics in thinking about the possibility of measurement of the two energies in question, *psychic energy* on one hand, and *kinetic energy*, on the other. First, Jung does not appear to see that physics itself is mechanistic when it boasts with the idea of total measurability that already at Jung's lifetime was no more unanimously accepted.

In fact, only by applying a strictly Newtonian, and thus mechanistic, standard in physics, we can say that all is measurable. However, within the world of subatomic physics, this paradigm has been seen to produce wrong or no results. This is so exactly

because *not all is measurable* or cognizable, and a large part of the phenomenology is based upon probability only, or, to use another term, upon *potentiality*.

Jung's problem here, it seems, is but his own mechanistic view of psychic energy. First of all, he starts from the premise that psychic and kinetic energy are *two different kinds of energy*. I would rather take the opposite approach and ask, right as the first question: 'Why should we assume two different kinds of energy?' To me, it makes much more sense in cases of doubt to start from the general paradigm that all in life is *one interconnected whole system*, except we can prove it is not.

When all is one in nature, we logically have to start from the idea that we deal with the *same* energy, that however may manifest in different ways. This is namely the crux that Jung faces here in his reasoning. He tries to find a common denominator for both energy concepts, something like a *unifying concept*, but then concludes that if psychic energy is like kinetic energy, then the psyche must be something that is in motion, as a mass in motion.

I think we can safely assume that the psyche is in constant motion, but this kind of motion is not one in space, but one in time, a constant change and development over time.

As time and space, as *relativity theory* clearly says, are intertwined, so must be the two energies, if at all we assume two different kinds of energy and not, from the start, one and the same energy manifesting in different ways. Jung concludes:

> If one is unwilling to postulate a pre-established harmony of physical and psychic events, then they can only be in a state of interaction. But the latter hypothesis requires a psyche that touches matter at some point, and, conversely, a matter with a latent psyche, a postulate not so very far removed from certain formulations of modern physics (Eddington, Jeans, and others). In this connection I would remind the reader of the existence of parapsychic phenomena whose reality value can only be appreciated by those who have had occasion to satisfy themselves by personal observation. (Id.)

These last sentences in Jung's reasoning on psychic energy are stunning in that Jung found a way out of the crux in which he seemed to be caught at the start. Basically, he says that it would be admissible to advocate both starting points, boiling down to the

admission of a unifying worldview that he, strongly informed by Platonic thought, assumes as a state of ideal harmony of all-that-is, and that he describes as 'pre-established harmony of physical and psychic events,' or its contrary. For the latter presumption, he then concludes that a kind of synergistic interaction of physical and psychic events, and their energies, could not be denied.

And to back his statement he reminds the reader of parapsychology, psychic research, a discipline that, as we know today, Jung was diligently studying, while at his time, it was less respectable for a psychologist to do so than it is today. In fact, having done psychic research for more than two decades, I noted over and over again that basically what we observe in parapsychology are *energy phenomena*, and to a much lesser extent physical, material or touchable events.

This was already an established fact in early spiritism research, the scientific predecessor of modern parapsychology. An eminent expert on the matter, Emanuel Swedenborg, namely was asking the same question as Jung and answered it by pointing to the bioplasmatic energy that produces, for example,

an ectoplasm; he called it *spirit energy* simply
because he had observed that spirits he encountered
during séances were emanating this energy, and later
found that same energy in plants.

There is a continuity in bioenergy research in so far
as all researchers speak of a *unifying energy concept*,
instead of splitting the cosmic energy into psychic
energy, on one hand, and kinetic energy, on the other.

Let me briefly report, for this purpose, the
explanations of Paracelsus, Swedenborg, Mesmer,
Freud, Reichenbach, Reich and Lakhovsky, and you
will see that these researchers did not have the
methodological scruples of a Carl Jung, and for good
reason. They simply focused on the phenomenology
of the facts that presented themselves.

PARACELSUS (1493-1541)

Philippus Aureolus Theophrastus Bombast von
Hohenheim, a wandering scholar and healer from
Switzerland, publishing under the pen *Paracelsus*, was
one of the greatest exponents of pre-Cartesian
holistic science, and at the same time a phenomenally
successful natural healer and alchemist.

He used to call the bioenergy *vis vitalis* and the ether in which it manifests and moves, he called *mumia*. He identified this energy in all plants.

Paracelsus was the first to recognize that the energy manifested in different plants in a way such as to form specific patterns, like a unique identity code assigned to each of them.

With this extraordinary knowledge that is, as I found, also taught and applied in Chinese plant medicine, he lectured that certain plants are collateral for healing and certain others not.

He thus proposed to take only the *vital essence* from plants, as this was later done by Samuel Hahnemann and Edward Bach in homeopathy, by use of a *distillation process*.

The tinctures he thereby created possessed the distinctive characteristic of being highly effective, condensed and potent healing agents through their *harmonious melting of various plant energies into a higher form of unison vibration*, which we have to imagine as some sort of composite vibrational code.

The same what Paracelsus did in the West, Chinese sages did in the East, as they found,

millennia before his birth, after testing over generations, that no one single plant can achieve a healing potency that a set of *collateral plants*, distinctly distilled into a super-vibrational tincture, can effect.

SWEDENBORG (1688-1772)

Emanuel Swedenborg, known for his research on *spiritism*, called the subtle bioenergy *spirit energy*.

Because of his specific interest in the afterworld, Swedenborg examined the bioenergy in ectoplasms and drew his conclusions on the basis of these findings.

As a result, Swedenborg lacked the comparative insights that the other researchers possessed, especially those elaborated by Paracelsus and Carl Reichenbach regarding the bioenergetic vibration of plants.

Swedenborg's concept however is well affirming that the cosmic energy is a *unified concept*, contrary to Jung's split definition that acknowledged it only in its dualistic consistence as *psychic energy*, on one hand, and *kinetic energy*, on the other.

Furthermore, as Swedenborg elaborated an entire cosmology, and thus a spiritual explanation of the spirit energy, he ultimately related the cosmic life energy to God, as a manifestation of the divine.

MESMER (1734-1815)

Franz-Anton Mesmer, whom I mentioned earlier in this book, was a German physician who, interestingly enough, wrote his doctoral dissertation on the influence of planetary energies upon the human body. His main focus was upon the *Moon* and lunar energy in its influence on various bodily functions such as sleep rhythms, secretion and healing processes. Contrary to Paracelsus' focus on plants, Mesmer's scientific and medical focus was upon humans only.

Mesmer got to his insights through the tedious study of hysteria and female hysterics. At his time namely, hysteria, most probably because of societal sexual repression, was a rather common emotional disease to be found with middle and upper class women who had suffered patriarchal and sex-denying upbringing and who in addition were living in a condition that did not allow them to abreact their sexual energy.

Mesmer's and subsequently Freud's etiology of hysteria was thus sexual, but Mesmer, in good alignment with the morality code of his time, did not touch the sexual question and rather experimented with magnets for healing hysteria. He came up with the expression *animal magnetism* for for the simple reason to distinguish this variant of magnetic force from those which were referred to, at that time, as mineral magnetism, cosmic magnetism and planetary magnetism.

He chose the word animal, and not human, because it goes back to the Latin root *animus*. In Latin, *animus* means what is 'animated' with life, with breath, what thus belongs to the animate realm. What Mesmer discovered was thus the bioplasmatic energy that since long was known before him.

Mesmer first encountered healing currents through huge and strong magnets that he placed between himself and the patient, and later observed, to his great astonishment, that the same healing effects occurred also without the magnets. Which made him conclude that ultimately it was his own body electrics, his own bioplasmatic vibration that had that curing effect upon his hysteric patients. To

conclude, Mesmer thus discovered the subtle energy that before him Paracelsus called *vis vitalis* and that Swedenborg named *spirit energy,* and gave it that somewhat fancy name *animal magnetism.* Behind the divergence in terminology, these scientists observed and reported basically the same natural phenomena.

Reichenbach (1788-1869)

Baron Carl Ludwig Freiherr von Reichenbach, a German noble who was a recognized chemist, metallurgist, naturalist and philosopher and member of the prestigious *Prussian Academy of Sciences,* known for his discoveries of kerosene, paraffin and phenol, spent the last part of his life observing the vibrational emanations and bioenergetic code in plants. He spoke of *Od* or *Odic force,* a life principle which he said permeates all living things.

Reichenbach was by no means a mystic, but an industrial and a natural scientist. His conclusions were based on the controlled observation of natural processes in plants and in humans, and the interactions between plants and humans. For example, when observing a plant in a darkened room in the cellar of his castle that he had isolated against

telluric vibrations, he observed, after having accustomed his eyes to the complete dark for about two hours, a blue-green shadowy egg-formed substance around the plant.

After having been certain about his own accurate perception and the proven repeatability of the experiment, he invited other scientists and lay persons to join him in his observations, and all the other persons, who were carefully selected in terms of mental clarity and sanity, corroborated his observation.

On the basis of his astounding discoveries, Reichenbach set out to heal sick people with the *Odic force* construing various devices for this purpose. He became very popular as he, as a rich industrial, went to the poor in order to heal their suffering family members.

Reichenbach's research clearly corroborates an important part of the spiritual microcosm of the native Kahunas in Hawaii and the corresponding cosmology of the Cherokee/Tsalagi natives in North America who almost exclusively use plant-contained bioenergy in their approach to heal disease.

— See, for example, Dhyani Ywahoo, Voices
of our Ancestors (1987).

REICH (1897-1957)

Dr. Wilhelm Reich was a physician and
psychoanalyst, and later orgone researcher, from
Austria. Reich was a respected analyst for much of his
life, focusing on character structure, rather than on
individual neurotic symptoms.

Reich was in many ways far ahead of his time in
promoting healthy adolescent sexuality, advocating
free availability of contraceptives and abortion, and
stressing the importance of women's economic
independence. Reich is best known for his studies on
the link between human sexuality and emotions, the
importance of what he called *orgastic potency*, and
for what he said was the discovery of a form of energy
that permeated the atmosphere and all living matter,
which he called *orgone*.

He built boxes called orgone accumulators, in
which patients could sit, and which were intended to
accumulate the bioenergy.

> —See Peter Fritz Walter, Wilhelm Reich and
> the Function of the Orgasm (Great Minds
> Series, Vol. 11), 2015.

Wilhelm Reich corroborated, through his research on what he called *orgone energy*, what holistic researchers before him already had observed: that life is coded in patterns of an invisible subtle bioplasmatic energy that is not to be confounded with bioelectricity, and that is somehow related to the creator principle.

> —See, for example, Wilhelm Reich, The
> Function of the Orgasm (1942), The Cancer
> Biopathy (1973), The Mass Psychology of
> Fascism (1933/1970), Selected Writings
> (1973), Children of the Future (1950), Record
> of a Friendship (1981), Myron Sharaf, Fury
> on Earth (1983).

LAKHOVSKY (1869-1942)

Georges Lakhovsky was a Russian engineer who emigrated to France before World War I. In 1929, Lakhovsky published his book *Le Secret de la Vie* in Paris, translated in English as *The Secret of Life*.

— Georges Lakhovsky, Le Secret de la Vie (1929), The Secret of Life (1929/2003), L'étiologie du Cancer (1929), L'Universion (1927).

He discovered that all living cells possess attributes normally associated with electronic circuits.

Lakhovsky made the discovery that the oscillation of high frequency sine waves when sustained by a small, steady supply of energy of the right frequency brings about what he called, perhaps for the first time in science history *resonance* and what today we know as *cell resonance*. He further found that not only do all living cells produce and radiate oscillations of very high frequencies, but that they also *receive and respond to oscillations imposed upon them by outside sources.*

This source of radiation was attributed by Lakhovsky to cosmic rays that constantly bombard the earth. Based on these insights, he construed devices for healing by the application of high frequency waves, that today we know as radionics.

— See, for example, David V. Tansley, Chakras, Rays and Radionics (1996). See also Peter Fritz Walter, Alternative Medicine and

Wellness Techniques (Scholarly Articles, Vol. 3), 2015.

Lakhovsky found that when outside sources of oscillations are *resonating in sync* with the energy code of the cell, the growth of the cell would become stronger, while when frequencies differed, this would weaken the vitality of the cell. From this primary observation, he further found that the cells of *pathogenic organisms* produce different frequencies than normal, healthy cells. Lakhovsky specifically observed that if he could increase the amplitude, but not the frequency, of the oscillations of healthy cells, this increase would dampen the oscillations produced by disease causing cells, thus bringing about their decline. However, when he rose the amplitude of the disease-causing cells, their oscillations would gain the upper hand and as a result the test person or plant would become weaker and illness increase.

As a result of these observations, Lakhovsky viewed the etiology and progression of disease as essentially a battle between resonant oscillations of host cells versus oscillations emanating from pathogenic organisms.

He initially proved his theory using plants. In December, 1924, he inoculated a set of ten geranium plants with a plant cancer that produced tumors. After thirty days, tumors had developed in all of the plants, upon which Lakhovsky took one of the ten infected plants and simply fashioned a heavy copper wire in a one loop, open-ended coil about thirty centimeter (12″) in diameter around the center of the plant and held it in place. The copper coil was found to collect and concentrate energy from extremely high frequency cosmic rays.

The diameter of the copper loop determined which *range of frequencies* would be captured. Lakhovsky found that the thirty centimeter loop captured frequencies that fell within the resonant frequency range of the plant's cells. This captured energy thus reinforced the resonant oscillations naturally produced by the nucleus of the geranium's cells.

This allowed the plant to overwhelm the oscillations of the cancer cells and thereby destroy the cancer. The tumors fell off in less than three weeks and by two months, the plant was thriving. All of the

other cancer-inoculated plants, those that were not receiving the copper coil, died within thirty days.

Lakhovsky then fashioned loops of copper wire that could be worn around the waist, neck, elbows, wrists, knees, or ankles of people and found that over time relief of painful symptoms was obtained.

These simple coils, worn continuously around certain parts of the body, would invigorate the vibrational strength of cells and increased the immune response which in turn took care of the offending pathogens. Upon which he construed a device that produced a broad range of high frequency pulsed signals that radiate energy to the patient via two round resonators: one resonator acting as a transmitter and the other as a receiver.

The machine generated a wide spectrum of high frequencies coupled with static high voltage charges applied to the resonators.

These high voltages cause a corona discharge around the perimeter of the outside resonator ring that Lakhovsky called *effluvia*.

The patient sat on a wooden stool in between the two resonators and was exposed to these discharges for about fifteen minutes.

The frequency waves sped up the recovery process by stimulating the resonance of healthy cells in the patient and in doing so, increased the immune response to the disease-causing organisms.

BURR (1889-1973)

Harold Saxton Burr was E. K. Hunt Professor Emeritus, Anatomy, at Yale University School of Medicine. Burr found that all living things are molded and controlled by *electrodynamic fields* and demonstrated to measure them using standard voltmeters.

He named them fields of life or simply the *L-field*. Beginning in the 1930s with his seminal work at Yale, Burr was able to verify his initial hypothesis of subtle energy fields that govern the human body. Burr set up a series of experiments that showed that all living organisms are surrounded and encompassed by their own energy fields. He showed that changes in the electrical potential of the *L-field* would lead to

changes in the health of the organism. By leaving some trees on the Yale campus hooked up to his *L-field* detectors for decades, he was able to demonstrate that changes in environmental electromagnetic fields such as the phases of the moon, sunspot activity, and thunderstorms, substantially affected the *L-field*. He found he could detect a specific field of energy in a frog's egg, and that the nervous system would later develop precisely within that field, suggesting that the *L-field* was the organizing matrix for the body.

In his work with humans, he was able to chart and predict the *ovulation cycles of women*, to locate internal scar tissue, and to diagnose potential physical ailments, all through the reading of the individual's *L-field*.

Student and colleague Leonard Ravitz carried Burr's work forward. Ravitz focused especially on the human dimension, beginning with a demonstration of the effects of the lunar cycle on the human *L-field*, reaching a peak of activity at the full moon. Through work with hypnotic subjects, he demonstrated that changes in the *L-field* directly relate to changes in a person's mental and emotional states.

Ravitz came to the conclusion that *emotions can be equated with energy*. Most intriguingly, Ravitz showed that the *L-field* as a whole disappears before physical death.

While Burr expressed himself in a rather misleading terminology, speaking of electricity when he connoted the *life force*, and of electromagnetic fields when it was about *The Field*, most of the literature on energy and vibrational medicine cite Burr as one of their pioneers.

—See Lynne McTaggart, The Field (2002).

In fact, Masaru Emoto says in his book *The Secret Life of Water (2005)* about Burr that he 'laid much of the basic foundation for the science of *hado*.' (Id., 139)

Summary

To summarize, these researchers saw the interactive link between cell vibration and health, or disease. All of them had a bioenergetic research approach which today we would call *systemic*, and

they are to be considered the first systemic researchers in the human history of science!

And all of them were able to construe devices or even work without devices to influence and manipulate the cell vibration so as to strengthen immunitary response and fighting pathologies. The process was particularly demonstrative with Georges Lakhovsky's research in that it was experimentally demonstrated how a simple device, because of resonance triggered with the cell's bioplasmatic vibration, could actively fight a cancerous tumor in the plant and thus eliminate the cancer.

Now, what my research on human sexuality is all about is to use this same approach, this same methodology, this same intrinsic knowledge about the cosmic and human energy fields, and the knowledge about the nature of our emotions in research on the moving, changing nature of human sexual attraction.

What I am saying after years of research on sexual attraction is that the present sexological and psychiatric approach to the sexual function must be evaluated by a sane mind as *mechanistic and*

incomplete in that it does not care in any way about *what makes us sexual* in the first place.

Modern sexology does not inquire in the bioenergetic nature of sexuality, and it does not inquire in the connection between emotions, and emotional energy, on one hand, and sexual longings, on the other.

When you read sexological research, you really gain the impression that humans are *sex robots* that once sexually programmed early in life, be it wrongly, are acting out a program, cost it what it will, and often virtually on the back of the partner that they jump and overpower like the virtual predator.

That's mythology, if ever, but not science!

Furthermore, sexology is sexist in that it never overcame Freud's well-known bias for the male phallic sexual function, to the detriment of the female sexual function.

Such an observer bias is of course symptomatic for a science that is highly mechanistic and linear and that is imbedded in a larger scientific framework where the cosmic energy field, of which our sexual energy is a direct manifestation, has never been

understood and integrated. Hence, I formally declare sexology to be *invalid* as a science in its entirety, a *pseudoscience* that uses phallometric measurements for assessing people's sexual attraction, which is a joke in my eyes because either a person is very spiritually developed and can voluntarily direct the blood flow in the penis, which would render this method completely illusory, or the person is very little developed psychically which means he can react by arousal to *virtually any possible sexual object*, and thus the method will give random results that, then, are taken for real. That's not only fake, it's completely inadequate when used against human beings in forensic psychiatry because it is unconstitutional!

In no other science except perhaps genetics so much humbug is being done and taken as official research than in sexology!

It is really time for a change, and the way to go clearly is indicated by *bioenergy research* both in the East and the West; that why I presented the various approaches to assessing and measuring the bioplasmatic energy in the foregoing text.

Summarizing, I can affirm that all methods and scientific approaches used for assessing, measuring

and monitoring vital energies converge in a single well-defined *scientific catalogue* that is so complete that it can be used as the basis for a new science, a science that integrates the specific knowledge about the human energy field, and that therefore is a functional, systemic and holistic science. In addition, sexology has never considered the *impact of emotions* upon our sexual attractions, and has from this blind spot assumed that sexual attraction was the primary mover, while the exact contrary is true.

It's our emotions that are determining our attractions; why certain *emotional attractions* become sexualized, and certain others not, is unknown so far. The principle, however, is clear already from the present bioenergy research: emotions are *bioelectric currents* that are movers and streamers in the organism and that possess their own intelligence and their own very interesting metabolism.

An intrinsic characteristic of this metabolism is namely that emotions change in a *kaleidoscopic manner,* and that this constant change is virtually programmed into them so as to ensure their healthiness, which means that blocking this natural

emotional flow results in various pathologies, sexual sadism being the most problematic among them.

CHAPTER TWO

The Huna Knowledge

Among native populations, there is a tradition called *universal doctrine* by Joseph Campbell and that is consistent with observing and recognizing the existence of a universal energy. In *The Hero with a 1000 Faces (1973/1999)*, Campbell writes:

> Briefly formulated, the universal doctrine teaches that all the visible structures of the world—all things and beings—are the effects of a ubiquitous power out of which they rise, which supports and fills them during the period of their manifestation, and back into which they must ultimately dissolve. This is the power known to science as energy, to the Melanesians as mana, to the Sioux Indians as wakonda, the Hindus as shakti, and the Christians as the power of God. Its manifestation in the psyche is termed, by the psychoanalysts, libido. (Id., 257-258)

Among natives, the Kahunas from Hawaii have an utmost of *systemic understanding* of the bioenergetic coding of life, and it is from them that the Sioux and the Cherokee of North America adopted it.

The religion of the Kahunas, as Max Long, an American psychologist, found in his lifelong research on Huna, considered the knowledge about *mana*, the cosmic energy, as a secret science. Long observes:

> It was a virgin field because, in spite of startling evidence of the powers of the kahunas (the priests and magic-workers of olden times), anthropologists had tossed their works and beliefs into the discard as 'superstition.' The Christian missionaries, arriving in 1820, disapproved of miracles performed by natives, and bent every effort toward eradicating kahuna beliefs.
>
> —Max Long, The Secret Science at Work (1995), p. 1.

Long found that these natives excel by their specific ability to understand human consciousness and the fact that consciousness and cosmic energy are basically one.

Contrary to our knowledge that in this field was mainly conceptualized by early psychoanalysis, the

Kahunas regard the unconscious, that they call *unihipili*, as a spirit force, and not as Freud assumed, as a trash container. And they ascribe to this force a certain independence of will and intention.

By its inherent will, this force, that they call the *lower self*, may stop collaborating with the other inner selves. Further, the Kahunas are convinced that it is the lower self that manufactures and handles the organism's *mana*, its vital energy reservoir.

At this point, Long spoke not only of *vital energy*, but also named the current or flow of this energy *auric charge*.

The idea that energy and consciousness are linked in some way is very old and it is some sort of intuitive knowledge. As Joseph Campbell observes toward Bill Moyers in *The Power of Myth (1988)*:

> I have a feeling that consciousness and energy are the same thing somehow. Where you really see life energy, there's consciousness. (Id., 18)

The *mana*, the Kahunas believe, is the vital force, the *life force*, and this force is being observed and attributed concise characteristics.

This force is said, for example, to be the constituent of all of the activities of the three selves. Max Long notes that the Kahuna priests teach that the lower self creates mana 'automatically … from food eaten and air breathed.' (Id., 10) He also reports to have found through slow and patient effort that the Kahunas' belief in the three selves describes each of these selves as an entity that dwells 'in three invisible or shadowy bodies, one for each self.'

This shadowy body is named *aka body* by the Kahunas, while esoteric sciences, as Long rightly remarks, use to call them 'etheric doubles.'

Long saw that the Kahunas use a *handy metaphor* for describing the *mana* force; they associate it with water as a liquid substance that represents the juice of life; from this basic idea, the Kahunas extrapolate the metaphor of the human being as a tree or plant, 'the roots being the low self, the trunk and branches the middle self, and the leaves the high self.' While the sap circulating through roots, branches and leaves vividly illustrates the nature of the *mana* force. (Id., 11)

The Essenes, the first Christians, interestingly had the same or a very similar imagery regarding the vital force. It was for this very reason, as Edmond

Bordeaux-Szekely found, that they had given so much importance to the water purification ritual. In fact, the Essenes spoke of a *Goddess of the Water*, a vital force that inhabits water and that can purify us through the use of daily cold showers taken in free nature, and with water taken directly from a source such as a mountain stream well known to contain highly pure water.

> —Edmond Bordeaux-Szekely, Gospel of the Essenes (1988).

Now, the amazing *water research* conducted by the Japanese scientist and natural healer Masaru Emoto fully confirms these findings with new and surprising evidence. Emoto found the enormous implications of vibration by looking at the vibrational code of water that he calls *hado*.

In the Japanese spiritual tradition, *hado* is indeed considered as a vibrational code that, similar to *ki*, the life energy, has healing properties and transformative powers.

Literally translated, *hado* means wave motion or vibration. Once we become aware of it in our everyday lives, Emoto showed, *hado* can spark great

changes in our physical space and emotional wellbeing. What he teaches can be called *hado awareness* or vibrational awareness, as part of a general acute awareness of how we influence our environment through thoughts and emotions. The point of departure is thus to recognize and acknowledge that in every thought and emotion, a specific vibration manifests.

Emoto's research was greatly promoted through the metaphysical documentary film *What the Bleep Do We Know!?*, but was started way before the great public got to know about it. These findings have shown that the crystalline structure of water can be influenced by feelings, intentions, sounds and vision.

In Feng Shui, only flowing water is considered to contain the positive *ch'i* energy, while stagnant water is deemed to contain a rather harmful and retrograde variant of *ch'i* which is called *sha*. The next amazing discovery that Emoto came about was that water has a *memory*—a memory far longer than our transient lifetimes. And third, that we can learn from water, by allowing it to resonate within us. Dr. Emoto writes in *The Secret Life of Water (2005)* that hado has

essentially four characteristics. They are frequency, resonance, similarity and flow. (Id., 33-35)

And this is equally valid for our emotions. They have a frequency, they show patterns of resonance, they follow the laws of similarity and they are in constant flow. Emotions have a frequency because they vibrate. They are *vibrations*, and their frequency is unique. Emoto writes:

> Frequency can be modeled as waves, a fact easily supported by quantum mechanics. All matter is frequency as well as particles. What this means is that rather than considering something a living organism or a mineral, something we can touch or something we can see, everything is vibrating, and vibrating at a unique and individual frequency. (Id., 30)

Regarding the lower self, the Kahunas believe that its *aka body* can slide into and out of the physical body and that it impregnates every cell and tissue of the body and brain.

The *aka body* is seen as a mold of every cell or tissue or fluid. It is in this etheric body, the *aka body* of the low self, that the Kahunas situate the emotions. They believe that love, hate and fear all come from the low self as emotions. By contrast, they teach that

the major job of the middle self is to learn to control the low self and prevent it from running off with the man.

In this context, it is especially of interest how the Kahunas explain the nature of prayer. They namely see prayer as the low self contacting the high self by means of the aka cord, which it activates, and along which it sends a supply of *mana* used by the high self in answering the prayer.

The Kahunas believe that our human organism is a spiritual microcosm in which the low self assumes the function of sensory perception; this perception then is presented to the middle self for explanation. The middle self is depicted as the reasoning self, what we today use to call our rational mind, while the low self's task is thought to be one of perceiving and recording.

It is said that the low self makes a tiny mold of the aka substance of its *shadowy body*, something like recording sound on a tape while all sounds, sights, thoughts or words are believed to come in patterns called 'time trains,' which are functional units containing many single impressions joined together.

More precisely, the Kahunas symbolize these patterns as clusters of small round things the size of grapes or berries.

Ordinarily, these microscopic clusters of invisible substance are thought to carry *mana* in that part of the aka body of the low self which impregnates or identifies itself with the brain.

At the time of death, the Kahunas teach, the low self in its aka body leaves the body and brain, and in doing so takes with it the memories.

The Kahunas' scientific spirituality is so refined that they even set out to explain phenomena such as hypnosis. They actually believe that hypnosis is a way to produce thought forms of ideas that are implanted in the aka body of the one willing to accept the suggestion. The same is true for *time travel* that the Kahunas explain as the fact that the entire *aka body* of the low self projects itself into a distance, connection with the physical body being maintained by a cord of aka substance. (Id., 38)

Finally, what is perhaps the most noteworthy scientific achievement of the Kahunas is their explanation of *memory*. They namely relate memory

to thought forms and explain these as *energy patterns* within the low self.

A number of related impressions is thought to make up a cluster of thought-forms, and such clusters are believed to record and contain the memories of complete events. (Id., 50) By the same token, those memory clusters are believed to reside in the aka body of the low self rather than in the physical brain tissues.

Max Long observes that medical discoveries have demonstrated that the aka of the brain, during life and consciousness, interblends with corresponding parts of the physical brain, and that openings cut in the skull to bare the outer layer of the brain in the region above and behind the ears, can be touched with a needle carrying a mild electric current, and, without injury to the patient, can cause him to remember and even live over in vivid detail events of his past life.

Long also reports about a device for measuring the *mana* current called *aurameter* and that preceded by several years the discovery of the human, animal and plant auras by Kirlian photography. (Id., 56)

Long found that the exact dimension of the *aka body* or aura of any living being can be made out with this device.

He observes that 'normally, the aka protrudes only a few inches from the body except at the shoulder blades and over the genitals, at which points the aura extends farther.' (Id. He also writes that tests using the *aurameter* showed that the spirits of the dead survive and live in their *aka bodies* all around us.

> Mr. Mark Probert of San Diego, a well-known medium, has a number of spirits who come to speak through him when he is in a trance condition. On this occasion, he went into the customary trance and a spirit spoke through his lips, carrying on a lively conversation and showing much interest in the Aurameter which was being tested. He readily agreed to stand beside the medium while Mr. Cameron tried to locate his aka body and trace its outline. He found it at once, and outlined it with as much ease as if it had belonged to a living man. (Id., 57)

Regarding the size of the aka body, Long notes a peculiarity that he says the Kahunas are well aware of, namely that the visualized *aka form* often seems to have grown or contracted very much, when found. The Kahunas, Long reports, believe that the *aka body*

could be made large so that it protrudes greatly, or so small that it retreats inside the body, and that thought forms have the same quality. (Id., 58)

In so far, Long observes, the Kahunas teach that the middle self plays its part by deciding what each event means and what its relation to other events may be—or, as they say, rationalizing it:

> The memory cluster of thought forms, once it has been given its rational meaning and significance by the middle self, is stored by the low self in the aka body. (Id., 59)

With the same amazing clarity and simplicity, the Kahunas explain telepathy, believing that '… the mana flows along the aka cord between two people who are in telepathic communication.' (Id., 61) Long pursues:

> The invisible aka threads or cords may be likened roughly to telegraph wires over which messages can be sent. They carry mana much as wires carry electricity. Just as the telegraph wires carry symbol messages to the receiving end, the aka threads can and do carry—on the flow of mana running through them —clusters of microscopic thought-forms. (Id., 59)

The most interesting in Long's research on the Kahunas' spiritual microcosm is the nature of the

mana force. He said right away that it certainly is *not* electricity of the electromagnetic type, and that it acts more like direct current of the type generated through chemical action:

> However, it is characterized by the fact that it seems to be a living force when aka body or aka cord substance serves as a storage place for it, or as a conducting wire or rod or cord. It has another characteristic in that it seems to find in the aka substance a perfect conductor. (Id., 62)

This is Long's report of the Kahunas' concise teaching of telepathy:

> In telepathy we have proof that the aka thread is a perfect or living substitute for a wire, and that the mana flows as easily over a connecting thread half way around the world as across a room. The popular theory that telepathic sending is similar to the sending of high frequency radio waves through the air, as in a broadcast, has been proven a fallacy. The radio waves fade and weaken inversely as the square of the distance traveled, and with a power plant as small as the human low self, a broadcast of this type would hardly be able to reach farther than a few feet. (Id.)

And it was 'with nothing but their *aka bodies* and *mana* taken from the living to fill them,' that spirits, according to Long, during séances, use up all the

mana in a single sudden effort with the result that the living can be lifted into the air, tables or even heavy pianos lifted, or even entire houses shaken as by an earthquake. (Id., 79)

In addition, Long writes, spirits could strike with *aka lasers* that 'would render the warrior struck temporarily unconscious, much as the mesmerist in Hollywood, by projecting a surcharge along the line of his vision—undoubtedly with a projected finger of aka-mana, and that could send a man sprawling to lie unconscious on the floor.' (Id., 79-80)

What is especially noteworthy is that the Kahunas know that the *life force* is effectively manipulated by the impact of consciousness. (Id., 86) As a result of their intrinsically scientific worldview, the Kahunas have no moralistic roof structure such as all our great dominator civilizations and they know only *one* sin: that of doing harm to another, and this also only in the case that hurt to another was done when *being fully aware of it* and doing it against better knowing. (Id., 91)

Yet the Kahunas' secret science is by far not the only source of this knowledge, while it's perhaps standing out in its detailed investigation and

presentation. Walter Y. Evans-Wentz, in his research on the fairy faith in Celtic countries, came across this knowledge as well.

Wentz observes in his book *The Fairy Faith in Celtic Countries (1911/2002)* that an Irish mystic and erudite on the fairy faith regarded *fairy paths* or fairy passes, the locations where fairies habitually appear, as magnetic arteries through which circulates the earth's magnetism. In addition, he reports that the water fairies are said to be kept alive 'by something akin to electrical fluids.'

> —Walter Y. Evans-Wentz, The Fairy Faith in Celtic Countries (1911/2002), p. 33, note 1.

Dr. Ong Hean-Tatt, a bioenergy researcher from Malaysia, wrote a concise study about the scientific basis of *Feng Shui,* the old energy science of the Chinese and concluded from a wealth of observations and discoveries that this science deals with the cosmic energy using about the same precision and objectivity as Newtonian physics regarding gravity.

> —Dr. Ong Hean-Tatt, Amazing Scientific Basis of Feng Shui (1977).

Dr. Ong establishes amazing parallels between Feng Shui and the perennial knowledge about the telluric force known as *geomancy*, which has a long-standing tradition in both the East and the West.

The factual evidence produced by the author that relates in detail to various UFO sightings and reports from reputed sources is dumbfounding and seems to prove the fact that these phenomena *feed upon earth energies* or telluric energies emanating from underground water. He also found that important religious cult sites, such as *Stonehenge*, are built exactly on the intersection of telluric lines. And not astonishingly so, it's around these sites that most of spirit, angels, ghost and UFO sightings actually occur, and for the very reason that these places are flooded with cosmic energy and therefore allow other dimensions to connect with ours through energetic cross-section and vibrational resonance.

Further, Dr. Ong examines the *bird migration* phenomenon and finds that it corroborates the evidence forwarded for the existence of the telluric world grid. Fact is that the birds more or less follow those lines and that the energy that emanates from them serves the birds as a navigation help.

On the same line of reasoning, in his conversations with Bill Moyers, Joseph Campbell speculates that all gods in all religions are ultimately but energy manifestations:

> [T]he gods are rather manifestations and purveyors of an energy that is finally impersonal. They are not its source. The god is the vehicle of its energy. And the force or quality of the energy that is involved or represented determines the character and function of the god. There are gods of violence, there are gods of compassion, there are gods that unite the two worlds of the unseen and the seen, and there are gods that are simply the protectors of kings or nations in their war campaigns. These are all personifications of the energies in play. But the ultimate source of the energies remains a mystery.
>
> —Joseph Campbell, The Power of Myth (1988), p. 259.

All the foregoing proves Wilhelm Reich right in that the human sexual energy really is the most direct emanation of the *life force*, the cosmic energy or human energy field that is the very creator force of the metaverse and of all life in it.

As we know today, the early Freud had the same idea when he came up with his *libido* concept; he

thought of the sexual energy as an ultimately measurable bioplasmatic energy; we also know that later in his life, Freud rejected his early idea, and it was perhaps from this moment that his theory of the *Oedipus Complex* became forged as a dogma while at the starting point, it was but a work hypothesis.

I am convinced that human sexuality can only be understood holistically, and systemically, and not through the *myopic view of a mechanistic pseudoscience* called sexology, nor through the cultural myths of Freud and many of his followers in the field of depth psychology.

And I am further convinced that what is most needed at this point in time is a conclusive terminology; we cannot communicate scientifically if we use one thousand different terms for one and the same thing. That is why I created the vocabulary, and here I do not bother if it will ever be accepted and implemented. I name the cosmic energy *e-force*, as an emanation of the *ultimate unnamable creator divinity* that I call *e*; and I came to call a future science of the bioenergy *Emonics*, which stands for *Emotional Identity Code Science.*

Sex, then, is an emonic expression of the *e-force*, and I hereby create a word that should have been created since long. We have the word *demonic*, but not the word *emonic*— and this is a linguistic perversity. It's as if we had only the word 'devil' (evil) and not the word 'god' (good). The original inflow in matter that is effected through the e-force is *emonic*, and its perversion into evil is *demonic*. This makes sense to me, if our Cartesian sexologists agree or not is not my problem. It's just as with modern medicine; they have defined what illness is without ever thinking to define what *health* is in the first place.

And that's the main reason they *cannot heal*, and that even the word *healer* is perceived as an insult by a medical practitioner today. I think we should respect their bias; they want to be businessmen, not doctors, they want to be agents of the pharma industry and have their share, and they are very little interested in the fate of human health.

And that's why we pay every year more for maintaining a healthcare system that rather is an *unhealthcare* system, and yet that asks every year for more victims. Slaughtered by death sentences received from gods in white coats. 'You have six

months to live, get prepared.' Once doctors begin to heal with the same effectiveness that they kill, we can begin talking about the beginning of the *Aquarius Age*, and not before.

CHAPTER THREE

Why Repressed Desire Turns Demonic

✳

Consciousness is precluded by *compulsive sex morality*. Morality and consciousness are mutually exclusive. Where morality is, consciousness is not; where consciousness is, no morality is needed. *Consciousness is the natural condition.* Demonic energies are the result of denial, of unconsciousness, of a blinding out of life, and the worship of what Freud erroneously called the *death instinct*. Reich clearly proved that what Freud called the death instinct is demonic desire as a result of a secondary drive structure that is in turn the result of repressed emotions, and repressed sexual desire.

Bioenergetically speaking, the flowing e-force in the body stagnates through repression of desire and then creates tension and strife within body and mind. As a result, all our thinking and feelings turns

negative, and emotions that are normally perceived positively, then are perceived as fear-ridden and explosive.

People caught in moralistic thinking in fact subscribe to a life-denying ideology. What these people worship really is death and destruction because their whole way of thinking puts life upside down and therefore is to be considered as simply perverse. Moralism is perverse, all compulsive sex morality is perverse.

Moralism came up as an artificial, hypocrite and pharisaical concept at that moment when humanity's evolution retarded and regressed when patriarchy started to prevail, around five thousand years ago. When compulsive morality was born, love was lost, and violence was becoming the single most rampant plague man ever created on the planet.

Aristotelian thought, impregnated by an arrogant and hubristic totalitarian morality was at the root of what I call the schizophrenic split of life into *erós*, the concept of erotic, sexual, physical and spiritual love and *agapé*, the reductionist, platonic, non-sensual and purely caring love that is deprived of erotic pleasure.

To begin with, I fundamentally question the concept of *agapé* and allege that it came about through a perception error, a distortion of perception, or the sheer *impossibility of perception;* a moralistic mindset erodes the memory surface so deeply that reality can only be perceived in a distorted manner; this is so because moralism distorts our body perception and thereby erodes the the thinking process, as in all perception the body plays an important part.

The division erós-agapé has been propagated philosophically by Aristotle and it's from Aristotle that first the apostle Paul and later the Church took it over and implemented it into their moralistic rules about the do's and don'ts of Christian living and loving.

What this philosophy overlooks is that *love bears its own morality* and does not need any additional 'correction mechanism' in order to be constructive and positive. While love naturally includes sexual passion, this does *not* mean that we feel sexual attraction every time we love somebody. But if we do, to do away with it because we fear that sexual desire may diminish 'true love' is exactly a moralistic and unnatural, and besides an *infantile* view of love, and

actually tears love down by the interference of intellectual *judgment*, of thought. Love is not thought. It is beyond thought.

When philosophy tries to 'correct' love, something is wrong not with love, but with the philosopher!

We all have seen and see every day what the destruction of love and its replacement by rigid *moralistic rules* all over the world has done to us: we are suffocating in violence, chaos, destruction and the indifference of our neighborhoods. This happened to us because we allowed pseudo-religious concepts to interfere with natural love.

With the same inner assurance that I knew morality would not provide the structure for building a new reality, I intuited that *only consciousness* could build the road to get there. From this insight I knew that consciousness can become something like the header notion, the hanger of the vocabulary I was going to create. And consciousness, I knew, meant *energy*, as you see it in the following graphic. (See it in full size on the next page).

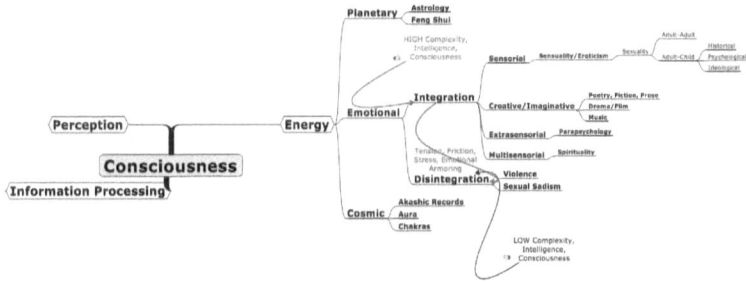

I was convinced at that point in my research that there is hardly any true understanding to be found in modern psychology and sexology for discovering what intrinsically are the nature of the human energy function and human emotions, and how they are intertwined in a 'field' of consciousness.

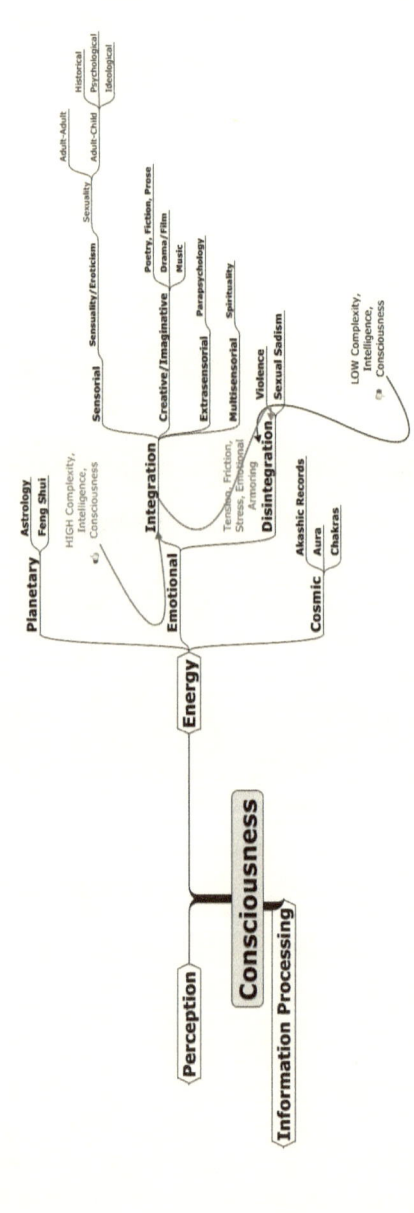

Freud's theory of 'sexual drives,' which, to repeat it, I consider to be a total error, is perhaps the main cause of the arbitrary and highly oppressive approach that the modern state in collaboration with psychiatry and security forces has taken since quite a few years to allegedly fight perversity. I wanted to bring up a rational scientific research discipline and accordingly, a precise terminology that allows to—

—1) Show scientifically that human sexuality is directly related to our emotional energy streams as manifestations of cosmic energy instead of being auto-executive drives; therefore, the human sexual function can only be understood when we understand the true nature of our emotions;

—2) Refute the belief that emosexual attraction for children is a sexual perversion, an assumption that twenty years of research showed me is wrong;

—3) Unveil the residue paradigm of an antiseptic and emotion-free sexuality as a Freudian myth and reformulate natural sexuality as a dynamic interplay of emotions *and* sexual desire, working in sync;

—4) Develop concepts of healing and care for sexually coercive desires and acts, and for sadism in both its physical and sexual dimensions.

My point is that without understanding our *emotional* life, we simply cannot understand our sexuality. This is why until this day the paraphilias were not understood by psychiatry. The reductionist approach of Western psychology and sexology toward human sexuality is hiding more than it reveals. Moreover, it splits off the fundamental unity between emotions and sexual attraction by declaring that sexual urges or drives were standalone unconscious wishes, and thus to be seen as independent of emotions.

I consider this view as one of Freud's fundamental errors. Yet, today's sexology and the greater part of Western psychiatry seem to run on this spur. Freud's belief that human sexuality was mainly a function of the acting out of drives is *mutilating spiritual wholeness* in reducing human beings to a robotics scheme.

Fact is that we are simply not sexual robots in the same way as we are not generally robots. We are human beings and our sexuality is human, and *not a*

matter of reflexes, automatisms, auto-executive behavior patterns, early childhood scripts, and so on.

Most people, when asked about their opinion on this matter reply that we could not know what was first, emotions or sexual drives? But this question is limiting our view on the matter because it puts up an either-or dichotomy.

There is seldom an either-or in nature; what we know is that emotions and sexual desire are impacting upon each other in a way to be functionally complementary. For example, when I look at human behavior and take examples that daily life provides, I see that—

—A nurse has an emotional attraction to sick people; as often heard, she will sometimes have sexual relations with patients;

—In homes for the disabled, once in a while headlines appear saying the educators in such homes had love and sexual relations with some of their patients;

—Many among those arrested for child sex tourism were teachers, pediatricians or child psychologists;

—People who work with the elder often have an emotional attraction to elders and they are likely to once in a while engage in sex with elders.

A childcare worker is first of all *emotionally* attracted to children and he may never think of sexual attraction, and even be 'violently against' the fact that adults have sex with children; and yet he is likely to attract a child that is so responsive that he will wake up one day and see reality with other eyes!

It will then appear perhaps as a surprise what is but logical, namely that all sexual choice is the natural consequence of *emotional* attraction—and not *vice versa*. This is a rule at least for most cases because it's a law of the emotional unity that has hitherto been overlooked. It was overlooked because emotions and sexuality have been considered as different scientific disciplines, and relegated to different scientific communities.

Emotions are studied by psychologists, while sexuality is the domain of sexologists; this split has brought about fragmentation. For what by nature is one, and that is split apart, cannot keep its intrinsic nature, its integrity.

Our emotions are intelligent and they are voices of universal consciousness because they contain e, the creator force, and are therefore to be considered whole, holy and sacred.

Now, as to healing sadism, as a result of the physical constriction that typically goes along with the psycho-emotional constriction of free sexual streaming, it is difficult to heal this affliction. To repeat it, until today, most psychiatrists keep affirming that it was impossible to really heal sadism while *palliative treatment* against the strong inner tension could be successful in many cases.

However, to contrast this negative and somehow outdated view, bioenergetics and various popular bodywork techniques demonstrate that sadism can be healed through helping the person to develop her full orgasmic reflex, and this mainly by dissolving the muscular armor around the pelvis and anal region and at the same time dissolving the blown-up superego by psychotherapeutic treatment.

To counter abuse, we have to put an end to hypocrisy and accept the benefits that more emotional freedom will provide us individually and collectively. We have to raise children in an

emotionally healthy and permissive way so as to foster their sensuality. Finally, we have to put an end to sexist ideals and raise children in an integrated way, a way that preserves the *anima* in boys and the *animus* in girls because this will assure a lucky balance of their *yin-yang* energies.

The problem of power and abuse, seen under this perspective, reveals to be a secondary problem as primary power for the naturally raised child is a by-product of his or her autonomy.

Power only becomes a problem when it is repressed, when it is thwarted. Love, too, has power, but it's not a form of power that degrades, abases and violates. Thus, the problem is not power but how we handle it. Power abuse then, is not a result of power, but of *depression*, the lack of power. Once we understand that, we understand all.

To demonstrate what I am saying with a practical example, I would like to comment on the teaching of the Indian yogi *Swami Sivananda* that is for me a quintessential vintage of a teaching that fosters sadism in all its forms and that is truly dangerous for our young people.

The teaching is to be found in a condensed form in his text *Practice of Brahmacharya* that is completely published on the Internet by its publisher, the *Divine Life Society.*

> —Practice of Brahmacharya, by Sri Swami Sivananda, Uttar Pradesh (India): Divine Life Trust Society.

I know that with my comments I may shatter and disturb the minds and hearts of many Indians, but I cannot care about that here; to consider such ideas as conducive to fostering public health is for me a sign of a *total perversion of values*, that is by the way all-to-typical for India, which is, after all, by far the most violent country in the world. And this text, and the tradition behind it, *Advaita Vedanta*, is at the root of this domestic, social and structural violence that has torn India apart several times in history and that is very virulent again, at this point in time and history.

It has no special reason why I have chosen that treatise on the practice of Brahmacharya, by Swami Sivananda; I just stumbled over it when searching something with Google. It is for me a good example, not more and not less, for spiritual and sexual fundamentalism of its worst. And that there is so

much of this kind today to be found everywhere has a reason! But it is not singular of its kind, and that is why I am using it. It is just more explicit but on the same line as Christian or Islamic fundamentalism when it goes to making down the nicest game of the world as an eternal sin and abject behavior.

Let me first elucidate that fundamentalism, in any form it appears on the stage of life, is *not functional thinking,* but the very contrary of it. What I call functional thinking is what in modern science is called systems thinking. These terms are synonymous.

The text I am going to analyze here is interesting because it gives the appearance of a functional approach to sexuality, and that is why it may attract some youngsters who believe it was in any way scientific and not just moralistic, while in fact it turns sexuality upside down.

Succinctly speaking, it demonizes sex at the very starting point of the paper, in the *Prayer for Purity.* It puts up not a question or inquiry, but puts an assumption or dogma, namely that being sexual means to be *impure.* It could as well say that God is an idiot. Yes, I think it is blasphemic to state that

nature is wrong, because it equals to saying God is an idiot.

This may not be a scientific statement proper, but I say it nonetheless here!

There are more assumptions in Swami's pamphlet that you need to be aware of so that you do not get wrapped up in the scarce yet absolutely violent logic of this philosophy.

There is a very important one in the *Publisher's Note* when he says 'our forefathers followed the do's and don'ts of the Dharma Sastras in meticulous detail,' forgetting to mention that *there were well fathers before those forefathers*, who namely did *not* follow the life-denying doctrine of Vedanta, but the pro-life doctrine of *Tantra* that was pleasure-affirming. He also forgot mentioning that Tantra lived much longer than Vedanta.

For you have to see that it appears obvious in this text that both the publisher and Swami imply that today true Vedanta is dead in India.

So ask yourself how long has Vedanta reigned? Not long, after all, compared to Tantra, and for good reason. Nothing that rules against life can endure,

because it is not pro-life (pro-god), but anti-life (anti-god).

And with this in mind, to speak of Swami as a holy man whose love to humanity knew no bounds, as the publisher writes, may be meant as a nice compliment and valid as such, but as an *affirmation of truth* it is invalid. He who shuns human nature and demonizes it is not a lover of humankind, but a hater of humankind, and he has not advanced mankind, but probably himself, against mankind and even more so, against womankind and childkind.

I know that there are in the West today not many people who can see through the veil of the pseudo-logical and pseudo-scientific assumptions in this text. Indeed, Vedanta, etymologically means 'knowledge,' and to a certain extent Vedanta is scientific, and much more scientific than Christianity or Islam have ever been.

So far so good. I have always admired Hinduism, and you can be sure that my remarks here are not targeting Hinduism in any way. The purpose of my opposition to this teaching has to do with *hygiene*, mental, physical, psychic, emotional, sexual and spiritual hygiene.

I simply say that the attitude and practice purported by Swami's teaching is not fostering hygiene but emotional and sexual chaos.

The *single best solution* for getting more children lust-murdered, more women raped and more conflict sown in the relationship between the sexes in general is to put up sex as impure and to try to regulate our emotions through strict discipline, behavior rules, and asceticism. It's really a demonic doctrine!

And before we go in some detail, let me affirm that I am by no means the only one who says that. You may not want to listen to what somewhat liberal psychiatrists or psychologists say, but what other spiritual teachers say, so let me cite two very reputed ones from India, who through the whole of their teachings have implicitly rendered Swami's murky doctrine invalid, or to put it more mildly, have shown the pitfalls of such a fundamentalist approach to human sexuality, and to spirituality.

These spiritual teachers are Ramana Maharshi and J. Krishnamurti. Both Maharshi and Krishnamurti have clearly affirmed in their teachings that the repression of emotions is the wrong way to spiritual enlightenment—or to state it more simply, that it is no

way at all to get there, that is represents a pitfall, a trap, and a delusion.

It is a *delusion* because it disregards and shuns the human nature: we do not become more human by trying to be inhuman! We become more human by being fully human, that means human with all our senses, and by accepting all our desires and longings.

And by the way, by suppressing our sexual longings, very clearly so *you are going to repress your spiritual longings,* because sexuality is the forefront of the longing for God. In shunning sex, Swami has shunned God, it is for me as simple as that.

This man was not a saint in my eyes, but a demagogue! And the truth is that India is pervaded today by this kind of doctrine that is utterly moralistic and anti-life, authoritarian to the utmost and very little enlightened, and this is the single one reason of that country's being trapped for so long in domestic, structural, ethnic and political violence.

While officially India may distance itself politically from extremist religious teachings, simply because that doesn't fit well in the business-attitude of modern consumerism, ultimately this is of no importance,

because it is all just a façade. The modern state presents itself smiling, but it's a false smile. India is the most moralistic of all nations on earth, and it's exactly for this reason, and for no other reason that it's the most violent country on earth.

To begin with, Swami comes up with the following statements at the very beginning of his text, three sentences actually, that I will enumerate, in order to better reply to each of them:

SWAMI SIVANANDA

(1) There is a great illusion in front of man. It troubles him in the form of woman. There is a great illusion in front of woman. It troubles her in the form of man.

(2) Go wherever you like—Amsterdam, London or New York. Analyze this world of phenomenal experience. You will find only two things—sex and ego.

(3) The sex instinct is the greatest urge in human life. Sex energy or lust is the most deep-rooted instinct in man. Sex energy entirely fills the mind, intellect, Prana, senses and the whole body. It is the oldest of the factors that have gone into the constitution of the human being.

There is so much already in these three sentences that I will need a considerable amount of time, energy and words to unveil the false assumptions, lies and hateful and destructive emotions contained in these simple statements, that for the non-initiated may seem harmless and innocuous.

Ad (1) The first statement implies that the *yin-yang* dualism that presents itself on earth to incarnated souls, through the eternal opposites of male-female, positive-negative, high-low, young-old, white-black, and so on, was an *illusion of the senses*. And here we are in the midst of Vedanta, indeed. What Swami says here is not singular and exceptional, but a regular and representative description of the whole of the doctrine of Vedanta, which considers life on earth as an illusion, a pitfall, a divine mistake, and an impediment to true enlightenment and spiritual progress. I think it is important to see the imbeddedness of Swami's teaching in the whole of the Vedanta doctrine because it will unveil a much greater relevance of this text. One may reject a Swami as an extremist exception from the rule but doing so would be a misunderstanding. The whole of Vedanta is extremism and, if I may say so, *moral terror*. Swami

is not in disagreement with Vedanta, in any of his statements; he is not original. He has virtually copied for himself, and in his writings, the doctrine of Vedanta, and gave to it a somewhat personal stress and access.

But I think for a Westerner to read this, it is important to realize that so far Swami is not an original thinker, but a strict follower of a strict tradition, which means he was an avatar of an ideology.

Ad (2) The second statement says not much about the world, but it indeed says much about how Swami *sees* the world. His worldview is what I call *reductionist*. He simply reduces the whole of living, at least with regard to modern life, to two terms, that are not even etymologically related: *sex* and *ego*.

Frankly, for me this is a clear projection!

When I read this I get a clear hint that for Swami, the most problematic things in his own life were sex and his ego. So in order to better cope with his precarious balance of mind, he needed to project these two problems upon 'modern world' or 'modern life' so that he could safely abstain from looking

deeper into himself and inquiring why in the first place he himself had a problem with both sex and ego?

Now I think it would be infantile to come up with arguments that try to enumerate what else could be present in Amsterdam, London or New York, or in the whole of human phenomenal experience?! Because it is obvious that life is much *more* than that. And if that was not obvious to Swami Sivananda, then, by all means, the one who got a problem here is the beholder, not the world, not modern life, not modern cities, and not human phenomenal experience.

Ad(3) In this passage of four sentences there are so many lies and misconstructions, that I have to go slowly, and bit by bit.

a) Sex is *not* instinct. That is the first important thing. If Swami had possessed real knowledge of sexuality, and was not repeating the misnomers of both religious ignorance and the ignorance of modern sexology, he would never have stated this in the first place. Sexuality is a result of our emotions, and it is as such a consequence of *choice*, or what I call *emotional predilection*. Humans have no instincts, period. The human being is not programmed into the

mere imitation of ontogenetic or phylogenetic patterns, but is free to create new patterns. That means sexuality is only a *conditioned response* in a society that thinks it has to condition sexual behavior, but not as an inherent and primal biological programming.

Sexuality is *not a conditioned response* when childhood is free, and when emotions flow freely. In this case namely, sexuality is clearly going along with *emotional predilection* and is directed by our greater spiritual wisdom, not an animal-like behavior reflex.

b) Sex energy fills the mind, prana and senses? Wait a moment! What a gigantic distortion of truth! The *sexual energy is prana*, pure prana, nothing else, not a different energy. There is only *one life energy*, not different ones. Then he says that sex has since long been in the constitution of the human being. But are we in Kindergarten? Sex is life, and life comes about through sex, no? Through what else?

From the next paragraph *The World is all Sexy* I pick out this passage to comment upon:

SWAMI SIVANANDA

Passion reigns supreme in all parts of the world. The minds of people are filled with sexual thoughts. The world is all sexy. The whole world is under a tremendous sexual intoxication. All are deluded and move in the world with perverted intellects. No thought of God. No talk of God. It is all fashion, restaurants, hotels, dinners, dances, races and cinema. Their life ends in eating, drinking and procreating. That is all.

a) How can Mr. Swami Sivananda possibly know what the minds of people are filled with? The world is all sexy, well, that is for me a nice statement, and I think if it is, we are all happy, and all is setup in the right way.

But fact is that the world is *not all sexy*. If it was, we wouldn't have wars and genocide everywhere in the world, and *rampant child abuse* because people would be busy with the nicest game of all. But they are busy with making money, and fabricating bombs, still better bombs, still more effective weapons that kill still more people in the next war.

b) The world is under sexual intoxication? Well, I think the author talks about himself here and projects his thought upon the world. There may be people

who are in fact deluded and move with perverted intellects, I agree. But *not all of them*, no Sir, this is again a generalization. It is all fashion? They do not think of God? Of which God, of your God, Mr. Swami? Of your mental image of a punitive and life-denying divinity?

Well, I am actually glad about the fact that most people do not share the *perverted puritanism* of a Swami Sivananda, because otherwise I am sure we would have had the overkill already long ago.

Fortunately people engage in nicer things than making life down and calling the creator an idiot, fortunately they are focused on beauty, on fashion and positive things, on good lifestyle, nice food, art and theater, cinema and photography, music and performance. Fortunately people enjoy eating, drinking and procreating. And fortunately, to be honest, insane individuals like Swami Sivananda are a rather rare vintage on the globe. I am really thankful that this is so, as it shows that most people are able to live a decent and balanced life, and not the life of a *spiritual terrorist,* even within a society that gives little guidance for right living, right acting and right thinking!

Let me take out another passage for commenting upon, while for the scientific reader I may apologize in advance that here we are entering the world of humor.

SWAMI SIVANANDA

Man, with his boasted intellect, has to learn lessons from birds and animals Even animals have more self-control than men It is only the so-called man who has degraded himself much by indulgence. At the heat of sexual excitement, he repeats the same ignoble act again and again. He has not a bit of self-control. He is an absolute slave to passion. He is a puppet in the hands of passion. Like rabbits he procreates and brings forth countless children to swell up the numbers of beggars in the world. Lions, elephants, bulls and other powerful animals have better self-control than men. Lions cohabit only once in a year. After conception, the female animals will never allow the male animals to approach them till the young ones are weaned and they themselves become healthy and strong. Man only violates the laws of nature and consequently suffers from innumerable diseases. He has degenerated to a level far lower than that of animals in this respect.

a) We are entering the world of *holy animals* who exhibit astonishing levels of self-control! Ever thought

there is a bioenergetic reason why lions copulate lesser than humans?

I could as well say that plants do not talk which is the proof they are stupid and non-communicative, while every shaman from South America will tell me the contrary, namely that they are very communicative telepathically. To argue in the way Swami does only betrays a *completely infantile mind.*

b) And then, what means *self-control* in the sense Swami uses it here? When I extrapolate this idea, it means everybody of value must eat only a slice of dry bread per day.

I think I can safely skip the rest here, except the passage when he talks about violating nature.

The comment I would like to make is that Swami has given an excellent example with this text, and perhaps with his whole life, what it means to violate the laws of nature. Further, about the practice itself, the author writes:

Swami Sivananda

The attraction for objects will gradually vanish if one begins to think seriously of the unreal nature of the world. People are burnt by the fire of lust. All measures that are calculated to

eradicate this dire disease should be initiated and put through. All people should be made fully conversant with the different methods that will help them to root out the dire enemy lust. If they fail in one method, they can take recourse to another. Lust is a brutal instinct in unregenerated men. One should be ashamed to repeat again and again the sensual acts when one is fully aware that the goal of life is Self-realization through the attainment of purity and the practice of constant meditation. An objector may say that these topics should not be dealt with openly, but should rather be talked about secretly. This is wrong. What is the use of hiding things? Hiding a thing is a sin.

a) Yes, the attraction for objects will gradually vanish *if one begins to think seriously of the unreal nature of the world.* And I tell you what, more than that even, the attraction to life will vanish in its entirety, and you will be close to suicide. That is what this practice will bring about: a suicidal attitude, and therefore I think it is criminal and should be prohibited.

b) People are burnt by the fire of lust? I think who is burnt here is Swami, not only by his lust but more so by his *guilt* of being lustful. This text is only apparently a philippic against lust; it really is a confession of

deep-seated and obviously, in his case, incurable guilt mixed with pride.

c) Sexual attraction a dire disease? Well, then, the author is blaming God for having created us as we are, or to put it in other terms, he shuns nature and thinks he can go beyond nature, and become superhuman.

Sounds familiar? I have heard much of that stuff, when my parents were telling me about the Nazi doctrine of the superhuman. It is well known that Hitler has used a lot of Hindu literature to stuff into his perverted philosophy, and the Swastika, the very symbol of the holocaust, originally is a Hindu religious symbol.

d) Now, the next statement, while it is again very general, incites me to comment because it is an excellent example of *demagogy*, in the style Adolf Hitler used it. The strategy is to combine a true statement with a wrong conclusion. For example, Hitler argued the country was in a terrible condition because so many people were unemployed. This was a true statement. Then he concluded that, because of that, the country needed a strong leader like himself to bring good order and new solutions on the

agenda. This statement was wrong because it projects a selfish desire for power; in reality, Germany could well have solved the problem of unemployment through an effective democratic government that was based on parliamentary values instead of single-man leadership. And here we go and hear what Swami has to say:

Swami Sivananda

In these days of modern culture and new civilization, in this era of scientific advancement, these lines may not be relished by some people. They may remark that some of the terms are jarring, revolting, offending and indecent and will not suit the people of refined tastes. They are entirely mistaken. These lines will produce a very deep impression in the minds of thirsting aspirants who are longing for liberation. Their minds will be entirely changed. There is no real spiritual culture amongst the people of modern society. Etiquette is mere show. Everywhere you can see much show, hypocrisy, pretended politeness, meaningless formalities and conventions. Nothing emanates from the core of the heart. People lack sincerity and integrity.

He justifies harsh judgments in this text by saying that he is ultimately spiritual and honest and that the whole world except him is *unspiritual and dishonest*.

The first part of the statement, namely, is true to some extent, namely that modern life lacks a spiritual foundation. I agree, spirituality is not a value considered important by consumerist postmodern culture.

But, the other statement, imbedded in it, is not true, when he says 'These lines will produce a very deep impression in the minds of thirsting aspirants who are longing for liberation.'

Like Hitler, he makes a big promise here, that is a promise to change the status quo through a magic stroke, by giving spiritual food and water to those who long for liberation. What he does in fact is to enchain those aspirants of truth, filling them with his half-truths and outright misperceptions about life and about the human nature, and that is why I consider his teaching as truly dangerous for young people.

And as I said before, Swami is not an exception; Vedanta is in itself an organized form of life denial, and it is really opposed to the original doctrine reigning in India for millennia, which was *Tantra*, and which was centered upon understanding life instead of judging life, and else upon beauty, the arts, liberal

sexuality, and permissive education that today has got almost completely lost everywhere in the world.

India could easily solve their inner and outer conflicts by effectively countering the plague of violence, but that is impossible if they continue to adhere to their sociopolitical neurosis, their judgmental mindset, their incapacity to put an end to the past and pardon their enemies, and their entirely life-denying views about healthy sexuality that naturally includes premarital sex, and an equality of women and children with men.

At this point in time, as I have seen it myself, and I have been in many countries, the situation of women and children in India is the most difficult and deplorable in all countries I have visited, and there is no way that under the present morality paradigm, women and children could even remotely have an equal status with men. And besides, it is still the rule that men burn their wives by pouring gasoline over them and burning them alive as a violent way of repudiating them when they failed in her marital duties or committed adultery.

It happens virtually every day in Delhi and other towns in India, and it is still the custom in the

provinces in India to burn women who have been repudiated by their husbands.

Such forms of *extreme violence* do not exist elsewhere. So, please, ask yourself why and inquire for yourself. It is a fact that the root cause behind all this is morality, and here at the forefront, sex morality or, to put it in bioenergetic terms, a perversion of the natural flow of the sexual energies through a rigid social paradigm that considers sex as abject, violent, animal-like and contrary to spiritual development.

That this view and the morality that it entails is against nature, is obvious; that it is also inhuman and that it fosters debility, not intelligence, is not so obvious. Hitler was a sexual cripple, and his level of intelligence, as we know today, bordered congenital debility. *Impotence, sexual aversion, extremist opinions and violence always go together!*

I have no interest to say anything against specific countries or cultures. But it must be understood what the future of humanity will be like if we allow the old ghosts to reign our future. We will be defeated, and not just with another world war, but with total destruction of the human race.

CHAPTER FOUR

Human Sexuality and Erotic Intelligence

*

Emonics, as a holistic science paradigm starts from the premise that our emotions can only be understood once we view them not as static and particle-like, but as dynamic and energetic, and in a constant flow condition.

The same should apply for sexuality. Sexuality is primarily a form of human interaction, and thus a specific way of how living beings communicate. It's actually a language.

Neither Aristotelian nor Cartesian science understood sexuality, a fact that had disastrous consequences on the drafting of so-called sex laws, since the *Code of Hammurabi*, from which time on human sexuality is regarded as a *set of acts*, a behavior that consists of penetrating certain bodily

apertures and sphincters and that is, at least on an underlying level, felt as aggression and even assault.

While the laws are silent for *procreative sex*, which would after all have to be considered in the same way, they consider all non-procreative forms of sex as basically flawed, dirty, yucky, misplaced, wrong, aggressive, violent, assault-like and criminal.

Apart from the fact that human sexuality is of course much more than penetrating sphincters, this traditional view of sexuality obviously is both negative and mechanistic and has little if ever to do with *real human behavior,* and the true reasons why human beings are *sexual.*

It's therefore not a surprise to see that emotions and sexuality were never really understood by traditional sciences.

This is so because the mechanistic neurosis in Western science only since recently is being replaced by an expanded holistic and systemic science paradigm.

Fritjof Capra writes in his book *The Web of Life (1997)* that with the shift from mechanistic thinking to systems thinking, the relationship between the parts

and the whole has been reversed. Capra notes that under the influence of quantum physics, we have come to understand that there are actually no parts in nature, but that what we call a part 'is merely a pattern in an inseparable web of relationships.' (Id., 37)

As a result, Capra reasons, we have to focus not on objects but on *relationships*. And indeed, when we begin to see sexuality as a form of interaction that can be said to be a primordial form of relationship, we overcome the Cartesian split that was pervaded by a subject-object view regarding sexual interaction, and that strongly marks the character of our sex laws. Then it becomes clear that the interacting objects in this reductionist view of sexuality were not human beings, but *parts of human beings*, typically a male organ (penis) and a female organ (vagina).

When we shift our focus to a systemic view of sexuality, we see that humans do more than just putting a stick in a hole, but that sexual embrace involves the *totality* of a human being, multiplied by the totality of another human being. Hence, when we want to understand scientifically what sexuality really is we have to consider it as a relationship and a

communication process, rather than an interaction of objects or bodies. It is amazing to see that when considering sexuality *as relationship* and nonverbal communication, our perspective and our feel of *being sexual* completely shifts to a new dimension, and it becomes clear that we can safely put behind us the negative spell that centuries of life-and-body denial have cast upon human sexual interaction.

Applying a systems view to emotions and sexuality will result in recognizing and acknowledging the *energy nature of emotions,* their constant flow, and their oscillating movement of charge and discharge within the sexual function. Such a new scientific regard on what could be called an *emosexuality* will also help us understand that emotions are ways of relating; when two humans embrace each other, their emotional bodies melt and their energies and bioelectric charges interact in many ways.

Please note that the term *emosexuality* as I use it is not to be confounded with the same term to be found in popular culture. To be honest, the term in popular culture namely connotes a form of sexuality where penetration is replaced by fondling and petting, which is how sexually immature,

incompetent, anxious youngsters behave sexually, because of their fear of the essential life functions, thus rendering them functionally impotent.

This melting of organismic energies in turn brings about a complex chain reaction of hormonal and other changes in body and brain chemistry, as it is demonstrated by the new discipline of *psychoneuroimmunology*.

—See only Candace B. Pert, Molecules of Emotion (2003), with further references.

From this different starting point, let us now look at the argument, another element underlying our sex laws, that sexual behavior was basically *instinct-driven* and could therefore be acted out safely only in the marriage bed.

Let us first look at emotions. It is true that our emotional attraction for a certain person or group of persons is not subject to willful control. It is most of the time unconscious. It just feels good to be with those we feel emotionally attracted to. It is something natural to be felt, something related to the heart, and not to the intellect, to intuition and not to conscious reasoning.

For example, when somebody affirms that they love children, they want to convey in most cases that they are emotionally attracted to children, and that they likes to have children around, that they enjoys their company, and so forth.

Emotional attraction thus is not an act of will, nor is it an automatic reaction; why, as a result of this impregnation, there is *sexual attraction* resulting from the emotional predilection in one case, and not in another case, is a factor that we do not yet fully understand, and that, for this very reason, we cannot predict.

To come back to our example. When the man who affirms that he loves children he may, or not, imply that he is also sexually attracted to children. And in case he thinks he is not, he may as yet nonetheless occasionally or temporarily be sexually attracted to children or a single child he loves. Or he may be randomly sexually attracted to children, or in exceptional cases and under exceptional conditions. He may even never have thought he could possibly be sexually attracted to a child until the day and moment when this happened for the first time.

Then, this will be a *novelty event* for the person, and they may react in various ways when confronted with the insight that they had felt sexual attraction for a child; for example, they may react with fright, puzzlement, bewilderment, guilt or shame, or they may laugh about it, or else they may just accept the fact without reasoning it out and without being shocked.

We do not know in advance how the person will react, and we do not know how they will act. The only thing we know is that acting out on the impulse is *not an immediate outcome* of the emotional attraction; and it is doubtful as well that it should be merely, as folk wisdom says, a matter of circumstance, a matter of opportunity for sex. This is well often the usual rhetoric but it is based upon projections. It is simply not true that humans do sex because they happen to be in one room together, because they are in a situation of power over another, because they can ensure a moment of unobserved intimacy, or because they have reasons to believe that they can act out with impunity, and will get away with it when raping child.

This age-old rhetoric is in truth a relict of ancient patriarchy and it is based upon a very negative view of the human male, and even the male generally. This view overlooks that people engage in intimate relations because, first of all, they are emotionally attracted to one another, because there is love, and care.

I think it is important that we pause here for a moment in order to clearly see that there must logically be a missing link, an element that we ignore that makes that *emotional attraction results in sexual attraction* in one case, but not in another case. What is this element? Or is it all a matter of randomness why one acts out and not the other?

My answer is that it is not random or haphazard what will occur, but that it is a function of *consciousness*, of emotional awareness. It is a matter of *emotional awareness*, that is, awareness of the flow of our energy streams in the body.

More there is emotional awareness, more there will be control and reflection, less there is emotional awareness, less there will be control and more there will be chaotic or generally unpredictable types of behavior.

In response to Heisenberg, Albert Einstein is reported to have stated that *God does not play dice.* Einstein did not want to refute the quintessential insight that, contrary to Newtonian physics, subatomic physics is primarily reigned by what Heisenberg called the *uncertainty principle*; after all it was Einstein himself who had discovered that electrons behave not according to certainty but on the lines of *probability* and that while they are by nature wave-like, they collapse into particles under observation, and thus under the direct impact of human consciousness.

What Einstein wanted to say, with this dictum, was that nothing in nature is haphazard and that there is thus a reason why things are as they are; and that we cannot discuss that reason away simply because we are not smart enough to yet see what this reason really is.

And regarding love, there is a reason both for the existence of love and for the way love acts and impacts upon our consciousness.

Love is an exemplary *communication process*, however very highly placed in the evolution of species, and therefore of extraordinary complexity.

Love and language are related. Without language, love would be impossible. But the intrinsic quality of love's language is that it is nonverbal, that it does not need verbal language to express itself. How is that possible? When you get into this, you will see how uncanny it is.

To explain love, then, as a mere exchange of energies, which is already an advanced view compared to 'putting a stick in a hole,' is still quite a *mechanistic* approach.

Let us see if an analogy helps us further. If love is a form of nonverbal or preverbal communication, then let us see if there are in nature other forms of preverbal communication.

One of the few modern thinkers I found who inquired about preverbal communication among animals is Gregory Bateson.

Dr. Bateson writes in his book *Steps to an Ecology of Mind (1972/2000)* that animals basically always communicate only about relationship(s). By the way, this fact is a strong indicator for the validity of the systemic description of reality as it seems to really be in accordance with nature's own 'way to think.'

Bateson gives the striking example of a kitten that is trying to tell us that she wants food. When we observe the sound the kitten makes to signal her need, we find that she uses the very same sounds she uses to address her mother. Thus, she will not really designate the item she wants (milk), but from her behavior we can only derive that she says something like 'Dependency! Dependency!' Bateson concludes:

> The cat talks in terms of patterns and contingencies of relationship, and from this talk it is up to you to take a deductive step, guessing that it is milk that the cat wants. (…) What was extraordinary – the great new thing – in the evolution of human language was not the discovery of abstraction or generalization, but the discovery of how to be specific about something other than relationship. (Id., 367)

If nature needed to take an *evolutionary step* for developing a language capacity as a pointer for all that is not relationship, then we can say that, by implication, nature really is from the start programmed in *patterns*, dependencies, networks and relationships; then nature really is a *Web of Life*.

Now, when we apply this thought to love, we see that love, too, basically is relationship, and *only relationship*. When we love, typically, we feel whole

and integrated, and our loving and caring feelings for the person we love, on one hand, and our sexual attraction for that person, on the other, *do not conflict* but are rather interacting with each other in a synergistic way. We can say that love is a sort of unifying system that links feeling and desire in a sort of constructive mix and allows us to care for another and at the same time have sexual pleasure with that person.

This is why we need a science that comprehensively describes the sexual function *as a form of complete erotic love*, that researches, without being overshadowed by a compulsive morality paradigm, the whole quite complex interplay of emotions and sexual feelings we experience when we love somebody. Emonics brings in the *erotic intelligence* that is missing in the modern definition of sexuality. In fact, the term sexuality has very little meaning because of its restriction to genital arousal or activity. That I why I coined the term *emosexuality*.

Emosexuality is a much wider term than 'sexuality,' destined to help cognitive psychology and science to research the nature and function of the loving bond between people.

In addition, Emonics builds awareness of our *emotional and sexual unity* that implies knowledge and acceptance of our natural emotional attractions.

To demonstrate what this awareness is actually about in practice and how the *Science of Emonics* can be used to functionally explain emotional and sexual complexity, I shall proceed, a bit like Krishnamurti, from negative to positive. While we cannot define love, we can show what is *not love*. After doing so, we intuitively will understand what love is. The same is true regarding emosexual awareness. Rather than rigidly defining what it is, let us see what happens when it is not. I will use a teaching tale to render the matter clear.

Let's imagine that educator Bernard F. is working for a day care center. He is a very dedicated and qualified day care worker and when he was interviewed and screened, nothing was found that could compromise his good reputation. He had a stable girlfriend, no criminal record and very good work certificates. He seemed to be the ideal educator and the children just loved him.

And yet one day, Bernard was found to have had little sex games with some of the children and everybody was horrified—including Bernard himself.

He declared that he had been 'overwhelmed by a sudden desire that formerly he was not at all aware of.'

Bernard is not an exception. Most people who are not trained in the perception of their vital energies are not aware of their emotional setup, and this is exactly why so many people act out chaotically and criminal laws are tightened without end—but with very sad results for all of us.

The law can do nothing here. We have to raise our awareness about our emotional setup and our psychosexual development— for it's a dynamic process. Only on the basis of emotional awareness can we develop some form of conscious and non-willful control over the play of our emotional and sexual attractions. All the drama that Bernard, the children and their parents went through when Bernard was found to have committed something society considers as extremely ugly could have been avoided if Bernard had previously been trained in emonic awareness. Bernard would have been *conscious of his*

natural emotional predilection for children and thus able to foresee his reaction in a critical moment where his emotional longings, sexualized, were getting the overhand. He could have interfered by applying ratio, restraint and wisdom, while not judging his desires as bad, so as to cope with the situation, and refrain himself as a result of his insight.

Now let's see what emotional awareness is all about. Awareness of what? Awareness of:

- Emotional attraction;

- Self-talk;

- Dreams;

- Feedback.

The first point in this little list may surprise already. I have written *emotional attraction,* and not sexual attraction, and for good reason. Bernard F. had a girlfriend and had intercourse with her regularly, and yet he engaged in sex games with the children he was caring for. To explain this seeming paradox, we have to focus not on sexual attraction as it says little or nothing about our deeper longings, but on *emotional*

attraction. Emotionally Bernard, as every good educator, felt deeply attracted to children. He would rather have changed his girlfriend if she did not like him working in early child care than abandon his profession.

This means that Bernard's emotional priority was primarily children rather than passionate love with an adult partner. (We all can perform intercourse without love).

When we look deeper, we can make out events, insignificant at first, that occurred earlier in Bernard's work history, and that were leaving him puzzled.

He was bewildered in some way, because children at times displayed a behavior pattern that not only Bernard would have to qualify as *seductive*. When Bernard recounted that later to the psychiatrists who examined him for the forensic expertise, they smiled at him: they secretly believed that Bernard was projecting what they called his *pedophile belief system* upon the children and that the children, in reality, had *not been seductive*, but were just carefree. The psychiatrists projected their mainstream paradigm upon Bernard's case and the children he was having an affair with.

The reality is namely that children who, as in our repressive culture, have no right to live their sexuality with peers, *do project sexual wishes upon adults* who are close to them.

They do this in a carefree way, it is true, but this carefreeness is not to be interpreted as an expression of sexual innocence in children. It is what it truly is, *emotional attraction and predilection!*

A real-life manifestation of the wholeness and integratedness of the child, and as such an expression of both carefree affection and erotic sensuality typically manifests as the desire to *experience closeness and intimacy* with an adult the child is enamored with. I do not say that this in all and every case includes sexual activity, I'd even guess that in most cases it doesn't. But in most cases where parents deny their children sexual freedom, they also, and even primarily so, deny to them, and this is significant, *non-sexual intimacy,* and the whole sphere of *autonomy* where the child can choose his or her friends.

Now, of course, the behavior of some children had to do with their *gerontophilic* attraction, but Bernard had no idea what that was all about. As these wishes

were unconscious, Bernard could not work on them and he could not do any conscious effort in handling them responsibly. This is the crux of this case and of many similar cases.

The solution, obviously, is not draconian punishment and blame, but *proper training* for child care workers so that they do their job with the appropriate level of emotional self-awareness of their emotional and sexual longings, even if those longings may be temporary only. After all, Bernard was a brilliant educator because of his high level of child-focused emotions. This is true for males and females alike because regarding affection and responsibility, there is no essential difference in a woman or a man taking care of a child.

The factors that may infringe negatively upon positive and responsible work with children can be present both in women and men.

One of the factors is emotional attraction toward children that is not embraced, but repressed. Emotional awareness helps us to deal with these issues. It is important to realize that our sexual desires are primarily generated by our emotional predilection.

For finding the *true etiology of sexual paraphilias*, I drafted, back in 1998, a self-test for finding out about the strength of people's emotional attraction and predilection for children. For this purpose, I looked intensely, and over some years, at how people who came to label themselves as pedophiles and how, at some point in their lives, they came to express and word their longings.

As a matter of fact, I became very early in this research aware of the fact that it was not by verbalizing their sexual longings that people express their intrinsic liking of children, but by emphasizing their *emotional predilection* for children.

Interestingly, I found that the more people were assured of the correctness of their attraction toward children, the more they focused upon their *emotional needs*, while on the other hand, the more people were only in a shallow way, and most of the time as a temporary matter attracted to children, the more they were inclined to talk about their sexual longings for children. This was one of the first hints I got toward recognizing that our attractions are first of all emotional, and only as an outflow from our emotional predilection, *randomly sexual*.

For the purpose of the test, then, I condensed the many statements that I had collected primarily from reports on the Internet, contained in web sites and poetic descriptions, or that were contained in autobiographies, into *15 Statements the Truth*.

I will not put up the whole of the test, as it is not of importance in the context of this book, but I shall publish the statements because they vividly illustrate my point that the etiology of pedophilia as a paraphilia is *emotional*, and only randomly sexual:

15 STATEMENTS OF TRUTH BY SELF-DECLARED PEDOPHILES

(1) When I am around children, I have an urge to have them sit on my lap, kiss them, cuddling and fondling them. When they leave me, I tend to feel lonely and often depressed.

(2) I long for strong fusion with children, to live something really special with them. It can be sexual but does not have to. The thrill is the *emotional closeness*. I desire having a special child all for myself with whom I can be in total symbiosis. I imagine this to be heaven.

(3) When I see children with their parents, I sometimes want to criticize the attitude of the parents, for often I find parents lack attention and even affection for their children. I cannot understand that parents have so little interest in

146

their children, so busy with their jobs, status, possessions or social life. If I had a child or children I would do it differently and have my children always very close to me.

(4) When I see parents hit their children in public, or when I experience this among friends, I get restless and aggressive and must control myself strongly for not exploding. Sometimes, in such situations, I am close to hit the parent in order to defend the child. It is a *visceral reaction,* and I think I could really knock down somebody if I did not hold back myself so strongly in these moments.

(5) I have an *almost magic attraction* for children. I attract them and they seem to attract me. When I a go for shopping or at the pool, there are quickly children stopping by, or smiling at me. They tend to meet me as an adult in some different way than they meet other adults.

(6) I experience often that children seem to trust me more or more quickly than they trust other adults, or even their parents. I do not quite understand why but it's a fact.

(7) I am feeling great and special when I am given a chance to babysit, care for or educate a child. It makes me feel good, as if I had more value then or as if I was more useful. I just feel so gratified when I can give love to a child and see that this love is returned.

(8) I have special relations with children and with elder people. I have more fulfillment in relations with either *young* or *old* people while I have few or rudimentary contacts with people my age.

(9) I have an increasing interest to find people who are truthful, honest and outspoken, who have not yet developed this rosy foam of hypocrisy that they smear in the face of everybody just for being adequate or social. I find children much more honest and I feel more rewarded in their company than in the company of any adult.

(10) In the company of children I feel more being myself, as if they could read my soul, my true being. Whereas among most adults, I feel kind of misunderstood, if I was an alien for them. I do not actually know if I am really so different or if I imagine this only. I think it is not so important after all to find out the truth. The important thing for me is that there are people who intuitively get who I am and who value me as I am. And this is in most cases children and adolescents. Therefore I have more attention for them than for adults and seek out being with them most of the time.

(11) When I am with a small child, I feel at ease, totally comfortable and very creative. I feel we can do wonderful things together. It's as if the world suddenly has become richer and more colorful. Sex is really not that important. It's just one thing among many. But when I feel that the

child loves me, the world is different for me, and life is again worth living. When sex comes into play, it's very exciting, but I would not hurt a love child just for having sexual gratification.

(12) I feel good in the company of small children. They just give me a sense of living. When I am alone, I feel rather depressed. I feel that nobody loves me. I find I am ugly and not worth to be loved. But with children, it's totally different. They seem to love me just as I am. I do not need to perform anything for them. Just my simple day-to-day being is what they love. This is a constant miracle for me, I mean that there is a way that I can truly be myself in this strange world.

(13) Without children, life is dull. Caring for those who really are worth it, that's what makes me feel special. I am almost an adult-hater, so to say. I tend to mistrust adults while children inspire trust in me, spontaneous confidence, and a feeling of belonging. As if I *went home to my true place* when I am around children. It may sound strange, but this is my reality.

(14) Emotionally, I can say that I need children and I feel they need me. It's just so fulfilling an experience and I am proud also that the parents make me often compliments about my specialness in my being with their children, which I feel is very rewarding.

(15) I desire *closeness with children*, to just be in my arms. I would feel so secure, so wonderfully

happy as I could never feel with an adult. I can say that I am truly *child-centered*. All what regards children magically attracts me while the usual stuff that is so interesting for most adults leaves me cold.

CHAPTER FIVE

Healing Sexual Sadism

*

INTRODUCTION

While in our culture, psychiatry seems to assume that either sadism is a variance of sexual attraction, and thus no pathology, or that it's well a pathology, but one that *cannot be healed*, my research showed me that sadism is well a pathology, but it can be healed.

First of all, sadism is not part of our natural sexual setup, which is naturally tender and accompanied by hot melting emotions. If you suffer from sexual sadism, that means that you are suffering from neurosis. Typically, in this condition, you will sense sexual wishes as *urges* in the sense that they are compulsive and explosive, and rather 'cold,' and linked together with violence, so that empathy for the

sexual mate *ranges second* behind the urge to abreact and explode sexually through the accumulated excitement triggered by more or less cruel acts inflicted upon the mate-victim.

Typically, when you suffer from a sadistic affliction, your superego (morality principle) is blown-up, which means that you are virtually *stuck in morality* and on the emotional level almost dysfunctional, unable to experience true empathy.

On the sexual level, you will be blocked emotionally and the streamings of your sexual energy will be inhibited by your muscular armor which is the physical expression of the emotional stuckness and rigidity.

The body always incarnates what is in the mind. If your mind is stuck and rigid, your body will become stuck and rigid; if your mind is open and dynamic, your body will be soft and alert, moving swiftly.

I argue that both the sexual and the nonsexual sadist need help for coping with their affliction. The way to go is to render the whole complex web of feelings and compulsions involved in these afflictions fully conscious, first of all, then to gradually get to

experience natural and tender sexual exchanges with fully consenting and mature partners, while practicing self-restraint regarding the sexually sadistic acts one longs to inflict.

Such a therapy or *self-therapy* needs time and progress will always be incremental only; there is really no quick fix to heal sadism as the original wounding that caused the sadistic response is an *imprint in the luminous body* and accordingly a groove within the neuronet that needs persistent effort to be erased, and a relatively long lapse of time to be made completely undone.

Sadism can be healed, but consistent work on changing the neuronet, the whole behavioral structure in matters of both erotic and nonerotic relationships, is needed, and the effort needs to be a prolonged one; this is why it is a good thing to be assisted by a facilitator or therapist, in my opinion, and be it only for encouraging you to continue.

Besides personal sadism, I argue that our society is as a meta group sadistic and has created quite a number of institutions or ways of group behavior that are to be considered as sadistic. For example, mechanistic science, with its discarding out of

anything human and subjective, anything irrational and anything emotional is deeply sadistic. Another example for societal sadism is 'child protection' as it is practiced since about the second half of the 17th century, and was institutionalized and backed by law enforcement since about the 1980s; in the meantime this paradigm is so much blown-up in the social agenda that it can potentially bring about major political dictatorship, fascism and tyranny, because the meta group consented to allow governments in more and more jurisdictions to unearth constitutional rights and habeas corpus guarantees based on unverified *hearsay allegations* of 'child abuse.'

The confusion is such that even the terminology used is blurred to a point that legal policy is messed up, punishing the violent offender with about the same sentence as the nonviolent offender when sex crime is concerned.

A good example to demonstrate this confusion is the notion of *statutory rape* which today in most jurisdictions is equaled in punishment with actual rape, while it's no rape at all, but consensual sex with an underage partner. From a policy point of view this is clearly the wrong strategy, for it does not

discourage violent crime by throwing the same draconian sentence over the head of a nonviolent offender that should be reserved for the hyperviolent offender.

If the criminal law system does not consider violence dangerous enough to actually reflect it in qualifying violent crime as more punishable, how can governments believe citizens could potentially become lesser violent when obeying to such kind of irrational, arbitrary or outright nonsensical laws? What in fact occurs is that each generation becomes *more violent than the former,* and this is absolutely logical within such a perverted and ungainly legal system.

The way out, as I have shown not only in this book, but in several other publications, is that sexual interaction be considered a form of natural communication and completely decriminalized and replaced by state-trusted *emosexual consulting,* while giving help and relief not only to the victims of sexual wrongdoing, but also to the 'other victim,' the person who mishandled their emosexual energies and became abusive in one case or the other —without however labeling a person as 'an abuser,' as it is done by now.

—See Peter Fritz Walter, The 12 Angular
Points of Social Justice and Peace: Social
Policy for the 21st Century, 2015.

There can be only acts of abuse, but no 'abusers;'
there is no profile of an 'abuser,' even if this is
ideologically asserted in most publications today. It's a
rhetoric on about the same level as Streicher's
pamphlets during the Nazi regime, which labeled and
publicly pilloried Jews as being 'sexual swines.'

We are responsible for our acts, and for harming
others, but we are not for that matter becoming a
'wrongdoer.'

The vocabulary needs to be drastically reformed
here to reflect any progress in consciousness that is
going to be made over time, in the near and far
future, in matters of social policy.

WHAT IS SADISM?

I am considering both *nonsexual* and *sexual*
sadism, because I see sadism clearly as a form of
violence, not a particularity of sexual attraction or
sexual preference!

Sadism is a pathological constriction of the bioplasm that is brought about not through too much sex but through too much abstinence, prudishness, sex repression and moralism.

Wilhelm Reich, as the first sex researcher in Western culture and some if not all sexologists after him have demonstrated that sadism is *not part of our natural sexual setup* with its hot, melting and tender emotions, but a constriction of the flow of sexual energies brought about through prolonged virginity, insufficient sexual contact and experience during childhood, youth and early adulthood.

The emotional blockage in sadism is not only psychic; it is not only manifesting through violent sexual fantasies, but more importantly what happens is that the lack of the capacity of deep yielding to the naturally streaming hot melting sexual emotions causes a *somatization of the psychoemotional constriction* in the form of a *muscular armor* around the lower belly, the pelvis and the anal region.

Typically, sadism lowers sexual arousal because the emotional flow is more or less blocked in the most sexually vital regions of the body.

As a result, when arousal occurs it is felt not as a nice hot and tender streaming but as a more or less unbearable tension that incites to a more or less violent acting-out, just to get rid of the tension.

When that happens, you will in many instances be afraid of your own violent urges and thus fear sets in which further complicates the already hot and explosive arousal situation. In addition, the orgasmic reflex is lowered in the sadistic affliction for the same reasons I just have pointed out.

The full bioenergetic discharge during orgasm is possible only in case the lower belly and pelvis muscles including the anal sphincter are flexibly relaxed, and not when they are constricted. With the sadist, typically, the orgasm is shallow, almost imperceptible, or it is so overwhelming that it causes a deep post-orgasmic depression, but it is typically not felt as a joyfully pleasurable body sensation.

Because of the physical constriction going along with the emotional constriction of free sexual streaming, it is difficult to heal sadism.

To repeat it, until today, most psychiatrists keep affirming that it was impossible to really heal sexual

sadism while palliative treatment against the psychosomatic tension could be successful in many cases.

However, Reich and other alternative healers have shown that sadism can be healed through helping the person to develop her full orgasmic reflex, and this mainly by dissolving the muscular armor around the pelvis, the underbelly, the eyes and the neck and at the same time dissolving the hypertrophied superego by appropriate psychotherapeutic treatment.

THE TWO FACES OF SADISM

As I mentioned above, sadism has two main branches, nonsexual and sexual sadism. However, this is only the outside façade of it because energetically there is no difference; nonsexual sadists repress their *pleasure function* in that they inhibit their sexual pleasure derived from the sadistic violence they inflict because of a still tighter superego as that of sexual sadists.

The sinful aspect of sexual pleasure in the moralistically highly conditioned psychic setup of nonsexual sadists makes them derive feelings of

power and dominance when they act out sadistically, and so much the more when the targets of their sadism are children.

World literature abounds of examples of nonsexual sadism inflicted upon children in the care of the Church, in monasteries, religious schools and even state schools when they are ruled according to a strict moralistic paradigm. Examples can be found in the oeuvre of the British writer Charles Dickens, especially in *David Copperfield*, the French poet Denis Diderot, especially his tale *La Religieuse*, as well as the author Robert Musil, especially one of his novels that was turned into a film entitled *Young Törless*, depicting the sadism of a group of youngsters at a military academy. They also can be found in autobiographies such as the personal story of Charles Chaplin.

I will restrain here from any judgment when discussing both forms of sadism. In fact, it is of little or no use to hear people roar about sex monsters when the next little girl is abducted, raped and killed, because these same allegedly so concerned people usually react with complete indifference when their

neighbor beats their child to death as a measure of 'strict discipline.'

So, where's their justice, where's their measure, where's their truth? In the first case we have a dead child. In the second case we have a dead child. That's why I think we have to apply a *functional and energetic view* for learning the truth about the sadistic affliction and its underlying constriction of emotional flow. Regarding nonsexual sadism, I mention the so-called chastisement of children, physical violence inflicted upon children for the pretext of bettering them. It is not of interest in the present context if and under which conditions legally the physical chastisement is considered by criminal law as a violent assault and thus punished as child abuse. I have done that in other publications.

As a second topic, I mention sadism in the form of violent sex desires involving children.

As the media today so often portray sexual violence only, we should not forget that physical child abuse and killing in the form of brutal corporal punishment is a major issue still in modern society that needs to be responsibly addressed by the lawmaker.

I think that both groups of people need help, those who have child rape, torture and murder desires, and those others who abreact once in a while their nonsexual pent-up emotions such as violent anger, rage and feelings of revenge using a child or children as the targets for their assault and in addition tend to justify their behavior as an 'educational measure.'

The way to go is to render all these desires first of all fully conscious; then, and only then can therapists assist in healing the sadistic affliction and help the client to gradually get to living sexual desire constructively; which means that for being able to help the client, they must agree and work hard on building sufficient self-restraint from inflicting long-lasting pain, mutilation or death to any sexual mate, as the primary condition.

Such self-restraint, while it is a *reasonable* measure in any case, is very difficult to observe for long-term sadists as long as the psychosomatic tension is so high that it interferes with and confuses cognitive processes.

If this was not so, all or great teachers of religion, goodness and morality would have since long

eradicated violence and abuse from the human race; unfortunately we must state the fact today more than ever before that imposed self-restraint in the form of moral teachings have made things much worse than they were and are originally.

A solution can only be brought about when we apply a *purely bioenergetic and systemic approach* and try to heal the root cause of sadism, which is the constriction of the emotional flow within the cell plasma and the aura.

The Sadism of Child Protection

This paragraph deals with so-called *child protection*, a highly controversial topic in international consumer culture because it negatively infringes upon children's education toward autonomy.

I openly criticize this movement's stress on protectiveness that bears the consequence of overprotecting children, thus crippling them for mastering life in a self-reliant and responsible manner.

On the other side of the spectrum, I wish to highlight the advantages of *permissive education* as an educational approach that deliberately reinvests the child's living environment with the natural dangers of life. It is a fact that in today's Western societies, children grow up in an *artificial space that deprives them of essential life experiences* and, worse, of important contacts with people outside of their family.

Modern educators like Maria Montessori came up with the idea of tailoring the child's living environment according to the child's age and size, thus segregating adults and children into worlds apart. Regarding the child's natural need of a variety of contacts to grow into a sociable and kind person, it is argued by child protectors that such contacts invariably endanger the child's health, physical safety or emotional balance.

However, people who, like me, have grown up largely unprotected and today are living overseas, will agree that in most exotic and shamanic cultures children are more sociable, more happily involved with a spectrum of experiences outside of house and family, more *responsible* and self-reliant, more helpful and far less naughty and selfish.

The *perennial educational paradigm* is based upon trust in nature and self-regulatory processes. It is still to be found in tribal societies. For this paradigm school has little or no importance because education is primarily bestowed upon the child by their parents and other members of the extended family. And yet, while these children live in a potentially unsafe environment, they are actually safer than children in most Western countries. For example, crime statistics show that in these countries, the number of child rape assault, violent murder, lust murder or kidnapping of children is minimal compared to the statistics for these crimes in Western societies. I give three examples for those cultures, Indonesia, Thailand and Cambodia, as I have lived in each of these cultures for several years, and I have seen that children are *more independent* there than in any Western country and yet safer; to be true, cases of child-related crime are very rare.

Western crime experts, justifying the Western child protection paradigm, tend to argue that these statistics could not be relied upon since the most part of child abuse went unreported in those cultures.

This is certainly a no-nonsense argument, and also an argument that is very difficult to refute. On the other hand, having lived for twenty years in developing countries, I can say that I have not heard or seen cases of such nature from personal reports or from local newspapers or other reliable sources in those countries.

This does not mean however that in these cultures there was no abuse; abuse does well exist in the form of ethnic riots.

In 1998, while I was residing in Jakarta, Indonesia, riots against the Chinese minority resulted in rampant physical and sexual aggression and many Chinese women and female children were raped and burnt by hordes of young men who, during this horrendous orgy and slaughter, shouted Islamic songs and Koran quotes.

The world press did not mention with one word that sexual violence and religion became thus linked during those genocidal attacks, which is another example for the *blindfolding approach* that journalists, worldwide, take in order to please their bread-givers. I would not have been aware of the details of those attacks had I not found, on the

Internet, a whole range of *testimonials* that clearly showed the let-the-swine-out intention of the organizers of these pogroms. Some brought forward evidence showing that a right-wing part of the military was involved in those attacks.

Whereas, when I studied in the United States twenty years ago, I was constantly reminded of *child kidnapping* when I received my daily milk, the milk box featuring every morning another child, with photo and details, that had been kidnapped within the last three or five months and where all search by police and intelligence forces had been in vain. And when I turned on the television, there was at least one moment every day when the topic of child abuse, abduction, rape or murder was discussed for the one thousand and first time. Of the many cultures I have lived and worked in over the last twenty years, the most unsafe country was exactly the country that most stressed children's safety and the need to protect children effectively: the *United States of America*. It is among all peaceful nations the country that shows, since many years, the highest number of child-related crime.

And this is really ironical since it was American organizations that came up with the concept of *child protection*.

From their alarmed perspective, one may well understand their motivation, but when seen in international perspective, their stress on drastically curtailing down civil liberties for the purpose of 'more safety for the child' appears insane. This contradiction between the reality promoted by American media propaganda and the actual reality in that culture is an all-too-typical feature of the hypocrisy in Western countries regarding childhood. The United States is only more extreme, but the *arrogant, hypocrite and know-all-better mindset* pervades all European and Western societies, actually a psychological relict of Colonialism. And what is childhood today in the Western industrialized world other than a schizophrenic split between the world of grown-ups, and thus of privileged responsible beings, and the world of so-called *kids*, and thus of inferior irresponsible beings?

The media, especially television and cinema play a major role in this false theatre, spreading the Western consumer value system worldwide, a value system

that by suppressing and criminalizing the most tender forms of sexual interaction between generations, breeds violence, hatred and hyper-aggressiveness mixed with *sentimentality* and a mindset twisted toward suspicion, mistrust, defensiveness and insolence.

The behavior of not only a large majority of Western children, but more or less a major part of all children in technologically advanced societies shows, as a result of *tactile deprivation* in childhood, the following pathological behavior patterns:

- ▸ Lack of kindness and lack of empathy with others;

- ▸ Lack of autonomy, self-reliance and responsibility;

- ▸ Clinging behavior, coming from symbiotic attachments;

- ▸ Strong egotism and 'difficult' attitude;

- ▸ Frequent anxiety, insomnia or nightmares;

- ▸ Strong materialistic focus, dependence on labels;

- ▸ Standardized behavior patterns and role models;

- School violence such as racketing smaller ones, etc.;

- Laziness, lack of attention, sometimes analphabetism;

- Depressions, drug abuse, sexual dysfunctions.

There are no quick fixes to heal these symptoms and, if there are, they do exactly this, they cure symptoms, but not the disease at its origin.

The disease is cultural, psychological and ideological; it's the puritan mindset that punishes pleasure and belittles violence, that roots out any spontaneous and creative behavior in favor of behavior that goes along with:

- The worship of idealized model leaders;

- Strong materialism;

- Possession thinking in human relations;

- Racial priority or missionary ideas;

- Humiliation instead of humility;

- Sadism, physical violence against children;

- Justification of slavery, civil war and structural violence;

- Revenge-oriented laws and violent prison system;

- Religion with a jealous, vindictive and violent god;

- Strong prohibition of premarital sex;

- Predominance of patriarchal values;

- Male inheritance prior to female inheritance;

- High regard for *yang* professions;

- High disregard for *yin* professions;

- and so on.

And yet, many United States citizens still tend to believe they lived in a liberal and free society, blaming the Taliban and other tiny minorities of acting out the shadow they deny to admit and realize in their own emotional and sociopolitical setup.

Regarding children's rights, their rhetoric is *suspiciously similar* to how the former apartheid regime in South-Africa talked about the black slaves and their social status.

All chidren's rights claims for a free, uninhibited and non-manipulated emotional and sexual life during childhood and youth are countered with arguments that deny children namely:

- ▸ The ability to determine themselves;

- ▸ The ability to make responsible choices;

- ▸ The ability to identify what could possibly harm them;

- ▸ The ability to develop autonomy;

- ▸ The ability to make friends;

- ▸ The ability to assert oneself;

- ▸ The ability to consent to sexual relations.

Before responding to each of those arguments in more detail, let me state what sounds a commonplace but is none: whoso educates children to become *clinging, dependent slaves,* whoso denies them to make responsible choices, whoso denies them to determine their private lives, their friendships and their emotional attachments, let alone lead their own sexual lives must not wonder that children growing in

such a restrictive mindset will exactly comply to the image of irresponsible, immature slaves.

This is why the propaganda of child protection is a mere *euphemism* and has hardly an empirical value. They are a front of ideologically fixated subjects who are forwarding as truth what is more precisely the manipulated reality they themselves have brought about through their paranoid mindset and the utter violence they unleash upon their children on a daily basis in what they use to call 'strict education.'

Of course, to them what they hold true is indeed true. Their ideological setup lets them see reality, and especially the reality of children, through a *distorted eye*. Their regard on children can at best be compared to the regard Czarist aristocrats bestowed upon their soul vassals. And their *protectionism* is an exact parallel to the protectionism a Russian landlord exerted over his soul slaves. The word *protectionism* says it all. It's a key to understanding the hypocrisy behind all sorts of so-called protection.

Some interesting parallel comes up when we look at another of those false realities: the juridical notion of a *protectorate*. In this term of international law we again encounter the verb 'to protect;' and here, too, it

is a pretext for colonial occupation of a foreign territory in violation of *Article 2 (4) UN Charter*, and thus against international law.

This term reveals that pretexting to protect another is often, even in the law of nations, a rape-like act targeting at violating the other and depriving them of autonomy and self-determination.

I believe that true democracy can exist everywhere, no matter what regime a culture or nation subscribes to, as long as it has a cultural and spiritual foundation that *respects human values and human life*. If we free ourselves from black-and-white judgments that divide the world in East and West, high and low, male and female, good and bad, and so on, and have a new and fresh regard on *education*, we have to acknowledge that it needs wisdom and patience. However, it is not given to everyone to be wistful and patient, which is the reason why, in Antiquity, teaching was in the resort of philosophers and men of high personal culture and integrity.

We can also highlight the problem from another angle. Where people need a captain, they are unable to steer themselves; where they need a right-wing ultraconservative child protection movement, they are

unable to protect their children within their own authority as parents, and that, excuse me, surely is a sign of *defeat* and irresponsibility.

And if we inquire why this is so, we get some keys about the true problems of childhood in our Western cultures. In my opinion, the reasons are:

- ▸ Disinterest of many Westerners in children;

- ▸ Interest of most Westerners in consumer goods;

- ▸ A lack of care present adults suffered in their childhood;

- ▸ Transfer of tutelary power from the family to the state;

- ▸ Lack of knowledge about what children really need;

- ▸ Hypocrite attitude regarding the facts of life;

- ▸ Lack of caring touch between generations;

- ▸ Lack of trust through disruption of the extended family;

- ▸ Lack of freedom for alternative forms of togetherness;

- ‣ Aggressiveness considered better than tenderness/care;

- ‣ Defensive emotional behavior because of lacking trust;

- ‣ Neglect of children's emotional needs;

- ‣ and so on.

This list is not exhaustive. It shows the peak of the iceberg.

If there is one area in modern society that is really neglected, it is *education*. The problem is that education is not human anymore and does not seem to be destined for humans, but for *robots*. Since we still are on the slave education level, what we've got is actually a *fake education*, a no-education.

With eradicating nobles, we have eradicated *true education* that, again not by chance, once was called humanistic.

THE SADISM OF MODERN SCIENCE

Modern science has to a large extent contributed to the impoverishment of education by its residual approach to life.

Modern science is not even modern. It was built upon what before was in the hands of the majority of church-obedient believers, not upon true wisdom upheld by heretics, poets, astrologers, witches and alchemists.

Modern Western science only recently began to gradually integrate some of the major insights of perennial science, thus gradually growing into a truly holistic science. And yet, even then, it won't be such modern a science since what we are going to achieve, by then, will only be what alchemists already knew more than a thousand years ago. Not to talk about much older sources of this perennial wisdom, such as the Taoists' holistic worldview and the hermetic sciences in Babylon, Egypt, Persia, India and other of the ancient high cultures of Eurasia that are five thousand and more years old.

Secondly, and more importantly, modern science is based upon a *residual concept of life* that, even though it has been questioned by quantum physics, still does not recognize that the first principle, the creational principle, is *energy*, and not matter and that matter is not different from energy in that it is only a specific condensed form of it.

Thus, what Einstein saw as a contradiction in observing that particles tend at times to be matter and at times to be waves, was an inevitable outflow from Einstein's observer perspective. Relativity theory was the first step in breaking apart the matter-principle that reigned since Aristotle, in the West, and quantum physics followed this line even more tightly and with seemingly more revolutionary results. But the first step on this redemptive path was the most daring one; in that sense Einstein was a true alchemist among modern scientists.

Despite the fact that modern science is presently challenged by a growing concern about our environment and the raising threat to our health and security, education leaps far behind the breakthroughs into a more holistic science.

If we enquire in the results that the restrictive, residual, anti-natural and anti-spiritual worldview has brought about in education, we observe that quality has been sacrificed for quantity. The quality of education that once was reserved for nobles has been sacrificed to achieve a minimal standard education for the masses. We have quantified stupidity with the nonsensical belief that stupidity for more would bring about less stupidity for all.

More specifically, in our attempt to bring about functional scientists and not intelligent or wistful scientists, we have developed an education for that purpose, an education that by restricting life to a mechanical concept brings about mechanistic functionaries and employees. That was logical since they had to fit into a mechanistic science, a mechanistic social system and a mechanistic religion with a single male Gee-Oh-Dee that one can please and manipulate by going to church, and else by falseness, sentimentality and generally a life full of taboos and restrictions.

We have to realize that education is dependent upon the reigning worldview and the reigning science paradigm.

Only *really democratic* governments allow an education that educates people to play the role of alternative elements within the mainstream system, thus allowing the existence of a *counterculture*. And where such countercultures exist, they do not only know and divulge the insights I present in this study, but they walk this talk on a daily basis.

Meanwhile, mainstream culture, unable to come up with creative solutions or cross-disciplinary approaches to the present complex problems in relationships, go on in their mix of cruelty and sentimentality, their focus on control and policing people, their lacking trust in self-regulative processes, their ignorance about the cyclic nature of life, their general fear of life, their pleasure anxiety, their growing violence and their utter ignorance about true, and not false and hypocrite, spirituality.

The concept of *protectiveness* is an important ingredient in mainstream's back-office and its strategy to control relationships instead of granting people the freedom, and the responsibility, to self-regulate their exchange processes with others.

And surely, protectiveness will not solve our relational problems, but in the contrary render them

even more complex and unsolvable, because these problems are related to how we use our bioenergy, how we handle our emotions. The more we bring in control and supervision, persecution and fear, the more we tend to block the natural flow of our emotions and the streaming of the sexual energy.

This is why awareness of our emotional flow processes is not considered by mainstream thinking as a positive value, and why people within consumer culture do not teach their children to become *competent sexual partners*, as this is done in healthy and natural tribal societies. Instead, our reality within the hypocrite present system is that most of us learned about sexuality in an atmosphere of secretiveness, pervaded by an overlay pattern of bewilderment, guilt and fear.

FAKE HETEROSEXUALITY

Our sexual behavior is largely the result of social conditioning; this fact has been found both by sexological and anthropological research; but what I am saying is that this conditioning is not turning us into sexual automatons.

Our sexuality, despite conditioning, remains a flexible, moving thing that is subject to change, and subject to conscious choice. I have observed that in most cases profound changes in sexual attraction are following up to previous changes in our *emotional predilections*.

As I have gone through the process myself, several times over the last thirty years, I know I am not talking about theory. I have lived in my life through virtually *all possible sexual attractions* for human beings. They were not cumulative, but one at a time, and for a certain time, more than just a few years, and they taught me important lessons, as the *feeling-level* is different when you love a woman, or a man, and then again different when you love a boy, and again different when you love a small girl.

The second reason, that is perhaps more important, is to be found in sexual conditioning itself.

I distinguish between *genuine* heterosexuality and *fake* heterosexuality. Ours is *fake heterosexuality* while the heterosexuality of most tribal populations is a genuine heterosexuality. What is the difference?

There are two factors: sexual experience and soul power. In global consumer culture, the child is generally not allowed to gain sexual experience, and as in nature nothing can be learnt without actually doing it, here lies the main reason why our sexual conditioning is not one that directs and conditions children toward heterosexuality, but toward homosexuality.

Regarding soul power, the same applies, and in fact, a sexually experienced person is always also a powerful, resourceful person. But as a result of a general denial of individual power and spirituality during patriarchy, we face in our traditional Western education not only a repression of emotions, sexuality and tactile pleasure, but also of soul power. The child is treated like a special race, addressed in a special language, wrapped in special wear, bathed in special tubs, given special food to eat and special toys to play with, and put in special houses called *Kindergarten* that suggest the child being a special person that is supposed to lead a special life.

This special life is a residual, not a complete life. It is a life namely deprived of many essential

experiences that every adult, rich or poor, goes through on a daily basis.

The most essential in the life of the modern child is lacking, namely *tactile and sexual pleasure* and the corresponding social coding that acknowledges and recognizes the *right of the child to be sexual* as a genuine manifestation of the child's soul power.

It goes without saying that sexuality cannot be built naturally when it is practiced in actual copulation with partners of one's choice.

What is built when sexual energies are withheld is *perversion*. This insight is clearly established and corroborated by psychoanalysis and sexology, but it also is a truth that a simple honest human being intuitively grasps.

What patriarchy tried to veil is the fact that it is not power that is destructive, but *powerlessness*, the very repression of power.

That this simple truth is veiled in our culture throughout most of human history is no wonder: it is part of what Karl Marx called the *Überbau*, a German word that can readily be translated as 'roof-structure.' Marx meant this roof-structure being of an idealist

and moralistic nature. It's the make-up that uses psychological manipulation, mass hypnosis or political lies to keep the masses from finding out the simple truth about the underlying socioeconomic base structure of society, which is the *real* social and behavioral regulator.

As it is with natural sexuality, so it is with soul power. It is not power that is destructive but powerlessness, thwarted power. Every human being who is conscious of their natural soul power is loving and constructive. Natural power is necessary biologically and socially for us to defend ourselves, to mark our difference or for building the courage to stand up for our preferences. How do you want to build your personal reality, with all that it implies, without this minimum amount of courage?

And for building courage you need a feeling of power! When you feel utterly powerless, you have very little courage and every day becomes a riddle with a thousand open questions. Should I do this? Should I engage in that? Is it not too dangerous? Will I not hurt myself when I stand up for my desire? Endless questions, hesitation, stagnation, procrastination, that's the result of such a mindset.

Without courage, without taking risk, you simply cannot live. Life, then, becomes perverted and you become a pervert.

What is a pervert? A pervert is somebody who has no power, who has so little courage to stand up for his values that he might throw a bomb in a church or rape a child in a public toilet once in a while to get a power thrust.

When you believe in this society's dangerous lies that are mainly brought forth by its *hypocrite moralism* as a defense against true and genuine morality, you have from the start lost your soul power, and your innocence, and you are from the start more perverse than by nature, and you are from the start more dangerous to any community.

Compulsive sex morality *is* perverse; it is the ultimate social perversion! The destructive thirst for power is not built in our natural emotional setup, but is a result of repressing our natural aggressiveness.

What happens when we repress the hot, melting and streaming sensations that a naturally self-regulated body experiences? Life cools down, our emotions cool down, our sexual desire cools down,

our appetite cools down and as a result our humanity cools down. Then we experience the cold rigidity of control, and love and compassion get lost along the way. This desire for *controlling life* is a by-product of angst, the fear of our own destructiveness.

And here lies exactly the logical circular loop, the fundamental error, because this destructiveness is not part of our natural setup but a result of our striving away from it because of the culturally induced perversion of morality into violent, false and smeary moralism. This perverse transmutation of natural power into powerlessness and sadistic control can be compared with the *retrogradation* of a planet that we know from astronomy and astrology.

When the spin of a planet reverses, which is a natural event to happen in the life of every planet, the energy of the planet changes as well. Astrology assumes that the naturally positive energy of the planet becomes negative as long as the retrogradation lasts. What then happens is that the planet's energy is interiorized and can only serve our inner or personal development, but not our social advance or recognition in society.

This image from astrology can be generally applied to the workings of the vital energies. For the positive and healthy development of a child it is necessary that the *élan vital*, the bioenergy, is in constant flow and that it does not stagnate, as it does for example in the case when sexuality is forbidden or experienced only under strong guilt.

What then happens is namely an *inversion* of the energy, both sexually and socially: the once heterosexually inclined child becomes homosexually inclined, the originally sociable child becomes a loner and the happy and adept child becomes an anxious, morose and inept child.

This is often the result of being punished for sex play in early childhood or because of religious prohibitions that bring about strong guilt and that can severely block the further psychosexual development of the child. The child then begins to think and reflect instead of acting joyfully and spontaneously and the creativity potential is more or less impaired.

At the same time the child becomes introvert and retires more and more from natural social involvement. In addition, it goes without saying that if the general tenor in a family is on prudishness and

pleasure-denial, the upsurge of sexual paraphilias within the next generation is inevitable.

By contrast, in tribal cultures where children can live their sexuality freely with other children, and where children are not physically punished, as for example in the *Trobriand* culture of Papua New-Guinea, perversions are practically non-existent. In this unique matriarchal culture, children sleep from about age three in special houses, where the parents are frowned upon to enter, and engage in promiscuous sex among peers from that early age.

The emotional and sexual maturity of the child thus is built *through direct contact, initiation, sex play and eventually intercourse with other children* as love partners. The parents restrain themselves to interfere in the nightlife of their children, and they are highly permissive generally as to the emotional and sexual needs and wants of their children. Children, in Trobriand, therefore develop a high level of personal autonomy very early in life.

In Western civilization things look very different and this since many generations, actually since patriarchy reigns, while we have information that

before that time children enjoyed a higher amount of sexual freedom.

Still in the Middle-Ages a pubescent child was considered to be an adult; marriage, for a girl, was at around twelve years and for a boy at around fourteen which was at the same time the age when a boy finished his apprenticeship with a master and opened his own workshop.

Thus still in the Middle-Ages we have a certain congruity between biological maturity and social maturity, or between sexual adulthood and social adulthood.

OEDIPAL CULTURE

And how is it today? At thirty still in pampers …, I'm inclined to say, somewhat exaggerating the situation, but I think there is a grain of truth in this affirmation. Today's postmodern consumer culture is based upon the Oedipal drama which coincides with the *Drama of the Gifted Child*, as Alice Miller expressed it.

Sexual experience is not gained but postponed; sexual energy is not discharged but retained and pent-up. Sexual maturity is a social utopia.

Despite Masters & Johnson's admirable sex research, we still live in a culture of emotional and sexual cripples, an insight that already Wilhelm Reich had and even before him Charcot and Freud. And not much has changed since then. Who is to blame?

Blaming psychoanalysis or Freud is like punishing the messenger for the message he brings. Freud has only analyzed and described *what is inherent in our culture*, and it goes without saying that the *Oedipus Complex* is a fruit of sex repression and completely unknown within the sexually liberal Trobriand culture, and similar cultures.

Freud knew that and he knew that Reich was right with his sex economy concept and his orgasm research, but his answer was that 'culture had to prevail.' That was Freud's literal answer to Reich. We have to ask today *which* culture did Freud imply in his answer to Reich? Is it a culture that mutilates nature, and that massacres the child's natural need for an emotionally and sexually rich childhood?

When we compare the Trobriand culture and quite a few other tribal cultures such as the *Muria* in South India, we cannot deny that following nature is the better way and produces the better results.

—See V. Elwin, The Muria and their Ghotul (1947).

What can we as a society, as a culture, offer to the Trobriands other than a daily soup of chaotic crime, violence, divorce, suicide, depression and raising cancer statistics?

What can we say about happiness lost!?

—See Jean Liedloff, Continuum Concept: In Search of Happiness Lost (1977/1986).

To sacrifice nature under a social system that we arrogantly call *culture* is truly insane.

A true culture obviously is one that is built in accordance with the laws of nature, and not against them. When we want to penetrate deeper in this problem, we have to look even more carefully at how children are raised in our culture. I bring this up not because it's my favorite research subject but because

you will find the key to the door to freedom only when you see *how you became what you are.*

Except you had exceptionally permissive parents and grew in a really loving home with lots of affection, and could live your emotional and sexual wishes and longings early in childhood, you have suffered, you have been made suffering, and this, to make it worse, *in the name of your own best.* And this is how you became a sadist!

If you have grown up like the overwhelming majority of children in our culture, you have been denied acting out your sexual wishes and you have accepted the strangely perverse deal they offered you for renouncing natural sexuality with peers, and be a 'good girl' or 'good boy' for your parent of the opposite sex. Accordingly, because you had no other choice, psychosexually you became more and more gerontophile, growing into a kind of ersatz partner for your parent of the opposite sex.

This means in practice that as a boy, you were supposed to fall in love to your mother, and as a girl, to fall in love to your father, and not only platonically! You were supposed to desire sexually your parent of the opposite sex and to compete with your same-sex

parent for being a better partner. If you did not turn with the wind and remained aloof to the social game called *Oedipus Complex*, you were labeled a schizophrenic child, and you were put in an institution. If you overdid it, however, and had actual sex with your parent of the opposite sex, you were called an oversexed child, and you were equally put in an institution, and your parent in jail.

And thus *whatever you did* had to go wrong in the end. And if you did as you were supposed to, and fell in love to your parent of the opposite sex while at the same time repressing this desire, you were not put in an institution, but you invariably damaged yourself, and became a timid, aloof, powerless, authority-craving, conditioned, sickish and dependent child, with one word a *modern consumer child*.

Let me get into still more detail, explaining how mainstream child psychology and pediatrics define and explain the psychosexual development of the child in our culture. First of all, let us see how these professionals define what they call *child sexuality*. The first thing to note in their rhetoric is that while it is agreed upon in all other areas of life that one learns something best when doing it, and doing it

repeatedly and thoroughly, this truth is put upside down when we talk about child sexuality.

It is assumed by those professionals that a child becomes individually corrupt and socially inept when having sex with peers during childhood.

By contrast, it is considered healthy if the child focuses his libido upon their parents and develops incestuous wishes. These wishes, then, are interpreted by the child psychologist as signs for the child's psychosexual dynamics whereas at the same time all is done to prevent the fantasy from being acted out, thus the child is supposed to remain with their wishes without however be given a chance to act them out.

In one word, all psychosexual growth in our society is a *fantasy game* that is lived out only in a fantasmatic dimension, and not in real life.

In addition, it seems to me that this theory is based not upon a natural discharge of the child's sexual energy, but upon its accumulation. Energy accumulation however invariably leads to an imbalance in the bioenergetic setup and brings about various developmental problems.

This is why some enlightened child therapists such as Françoise Dolto (1908-1988) in France, while generally agreeing with our society's stance to forbid child-child sexual activity, conceded that the *Oedipus Complex* as it is part of our culture's child-rearing paradigm, breeds a real danger of incest and thus should be corrected in some way. When, back in 1986, I questioned Dr. Dolto on this point with the idea that perhaps some forms of sexual interaction *should be allowed socially* between children and other adults than their parents, she was generally in favor of such an idea and said that these adults, preferably educators of the child, could then safely bear the incestuous charge the child would project upon them. However, she felt that, while cuddling and fantasy sex in a game-like setting was good and healthy in such a situation, a *real sexual interaction* between educators and the children they cared for could neither be allowed psychologically nor socially for the best of the child. Upon my reply that, then, the child in last resort in our culture was paying the bill for maintaining a compulsive sex morality paradigm that belongs to the past, she agreed and sadly added that this was our cultural heritage and that she, as a psychoanalyst, was not having the task of triggering a

'cultural revolution,' as that would be a matter for politicians and parliaments to decide upon.

Thus, child sex is clearly a matter of social politics and not a matter of psychology and still less of sexology!

That we more or less *all have been mutilated* in our psychosexual setup through the harsh prohibition of living our child sexuality healthily in an anti-life culture is thus something that is not even hidden anymore, but openly admitted by child psychology practitioners of high caliber.

Apart from the abstruse logic and perversity of such a child-rearing paradigm, that actually sacrifices the child's best years for maintaining a life-denying culture, statistics speak a clear language. With the Trobriands, the divorce rate is about four percent, in some regions in our Western society it is growing beyond seventy-five percent. While the Trobriands' sexuality is healthy and almost totally free of sexual perversions, in our societies more than one third of the population is in continuous psychotherapeutic treatment because of emotional and sexual disturbances, frenetic partner change, frigidity,

narcissism or impotence or corresponding problems within the couple.

The child is sacrificed as a scapegoat for society to be able to maintain its moralistic network of lies and so-called religious assumptions or beliefs.

Every single child who is forced to abnegate their sexuality during childhood and youth pays the price of emotional and sexual dysfunctions for lifetime! This is brought about through a process that Freud called *identification*, and through social hypnosis and the early conditioning of the child with industrially fabricated toys. These toys, because they have no natural associative quality with the human body, alienate children gradually from their bodies.

Regarding identification, the rhetoric in child psychology is that it is natural for a boy to wanting to become like his father and for a girl like her mother. The truth is of course that down the road we want to become *ourselves* and not tin soldiers modeled and cloned after our parents.

But this fact is of course occulted because it's not politically correct to bring that up in a *culture of imitation* and industrial manipulation in which the

individual is legitimate only in his or her capacity as a consumer, and not in their autonomy as a self-thinker and self-feeler. The first identification is called *homosexual:* the child identifies with the same-sex parent, during the so-called anal phase. Next comes the *heterosexual* identification with the parent of the opposite sex, during the genital phase, and here Freud spoke of the so-called Oedipal phase or *Oedipus Complex.*

Thus, if we think this through until the end, we are potentially all homosexual because our society denies child sexuality! This latent homosexuality in our culture is the result of *psychosexual manipulation* from early childhood, and not a natural component of the sex drive.

It's not a coincidence that the largest homosexual organizations are in the United States which is the country where the repression of the child's natural sexuality has been the toughest one since the times of the Inquisition. This should, then, be a wake-up call for all of you who still believe that things are more or less okay as they are in modern consumer culture, and that we can go on with this mess, if we only bring up new laws every month, new anti-childsex campaigns

every year and new anti-pornography laws every decade. No, we cannot fool nature without bringing about nothing less but a sociopolitical catastrophe and an ecopolitical disaster.

Not nature is wrong but the way we have handled nature during the last thousand years of dull and stupid patriarchy, the way we have distorted nature, wanting to be smarter than its creator! What a hubris!

THE CULTURAL CHILD SEX DOGMA

Our sex laws are made to protect the cultural bias and choice that denies children their free emotions and sexuality. These laws, today more than ever before, are enforced ruthlessly, and without having a deeper look at the human damage that is done when sensitive matters are handled by insensitive people.

Sex laws and their enforcement do not bring solutions, but actually make things worse; we tend to think that all is in good hands when we give it over into the care of our police, who are people that have been demonstrated to come often from abusive and violent backgrounds, and who have for the most part

never received an education to true sensuality, empathy and intelligence.

To let police regulate our loves and likes is really suicidal for every democratic society, and it's quite unbelievable that this truth never seems to enter the heads of our political leaders, which shows, more than anything, their residual level of intelligence. Instead we go on finding it okay that children are from birth psychosexually distorted and fantasy-mated with their parents in an incestuous nightmare of gigantic dimensions!

Something must be wrong here, wrong from the start. We created the ultimate incest scenario and established it as a cultural credo, while at the same time affirming we held incest as immoral and abject.

But that this incest is acted out sexually is of no importance! The social conditioning is brought about exactly because this incest is imaginary and its acting out repressed, and the damage done to the child's psyche comes neither from natural sex nor from incest sex, but from the *contradiction of creating a desire and at the same time prohibiting its realization* because this is a schizoid behavior.

And we cannot raise mentally healthy children with schizoid formulas. It's impossible.

What we have created is *emotional abuse* and this is the really destructive form of incest anyway; it is destructive because it acts contrary to the child's natural striving for autonomy, and because it is sanctified by the patriarchal authority principle and obsessive consumption!

The so-called Oedipal phase of the psychosexual development of the child that takes generally place between the 5th and 7th years of life is set out to heterosexualize the child's originally homoerotic sexuality through psychosexual attraction toward the parent of the opposite sex.

This is how it is set out in the theory. If it works like that in real life is another question.

In this system heterosexuality is brought about only if the child has successfully gone through both identifications because only in this case the child can gradually end the psychic symbiosis with the matrix and really build an individual character structure.

It is obvious that our cultural concept of heterosexuality is in reality based upon an atrocious

misconception and manipulation of nature; it is for this reason why this artificial heterosexuality is rather fragile. Natural heterosexuality is something entirely different! It is a heterosexuality that I would qualify as *developmental* rather than *normative.*

It comes about through deep affectionate friendship, love and natural promiscuous intercourse with partners of the other sex, and this especially during early childhood, and again later on during adolescence.

Our Western concept of 'heterosexuality' is basically *schizoid.* It is based upon the early homosexual and gerontophile conditioning of the child that, to make it worse, is forced upon the child, while declaring this perverse manipulation arrogantly the normal psychosexual development of the child. I have once told a little boy about it and he understood immediately and replied:

> I know, but I won't collaborate. Let them come! I won't play their perverse game. They definitely love dogs more than children! And when they love children, they love us only as lightning catchers. Because they can't even get along with each other, among adults, and when they are running amok, it's us, the children, who will get the beating, invariably so!

Once we begin to understand life as a dynamic sequence of processes and an outcome of probability, we cannot but affirm that it is more probable than not that a child gets stuck in the Oedipus rather than liquidating it. For example, it's *almost impossible* for a child to liquidate his Oedipus when the parent of the opposite sex is either dead, absent or unacceptable as a role model. And it's a social fact that the number of single-parent families increases every year, especially in huge urban areas around the world.

One consequence of this fact is that the psychosexual development of the child becomes more and more distorted, if not perverted. A lacking father is a lacking father, do what you will and since society violently opposes the possibility of childless couples or neighbors assuming the fathering role for children they love, many children today are left with a considerable emotional and tactile vacuum that society is absolutely unable to fill. And if the mother tries to replace the father, things get even worse.

Such a *neurotic mother* then becomes a sadistic and phallic bitch who castrates and handicaps her children even more thoroughly.

What generally happens in this constellation is that the sexual energy in the child inverts: it begins to be oriented *inward* instead of naturally outward; it shifts its spin, so to say, and retrogrades. The consequence is that the child retreats, and becomes *timid, anxious, dependent, clinging, passive* and *authority-craving,* or in the contrary mean, vulgar and rebellious. If not other factors act counter to the inversion of the bioenergy, the child becomes *homosexual.*

This is then, the logical deal that is part of the system. For the child who was unable to perform the master jump into *fake heterosexuality* that was the reward for liquidating the Oedipus, thus remains on the anal-sadistic level of psychosexual development.

Rape vs. Loving Embrace

And on this anal-sadistic level are situated most people in our culture, as very few have really liquidated their Oedipus and went beyond homosexual identification and into full genitality.

Every bioenergetic practitioner will confirm Reich's saying that our culture is one of sexual cripples! True

genitality exists only at a tiny percentage, while on the Trobriand islands and in other permissive tribal cultures it's the majority!

When the child gets stuck in the Oedipus or, with other words, remains fixated at the homosexual identification level, what happens is that the fusion with the matrix gets reactivated as a kind of secondary fusion, and is then perpetuated into adolescence where it is fueled by higher sexual energy. At the same time, nonsexual emotions such as rage and feelings of revenge against parents and establishment get heated up and become linked to the sexual charge. This is how violent rape urges are created in the first place!

In addition, the *retrograde negative sexual energy* attracts equally negative emotional energy from the social environment, peers and groupings which explains the fact of what we call 'adolescent revolt.'

My point here is that this revolt is by no means a natural or developmental necessity, but in the contrary a revolt against the sordid sadistic repression of the child's natural sex drive during the first decade of the child's life! And further, this revolt is the beginning of the *violent rape urges* that characterize

homo normalis in so-called civilized culture. These urges, for the most part, are acted out with prostitutes or prostitute children, otherwise, as most reports show, secretly with children in the extended family, or with employees or their children, or otherwise with people who are socially in an inferior position as oneself so that they have limited chances to revolt against violent sexual domination.

What I am saying is that all this is part of the system in a society that denies child-child sex and thus nothing to make a scandal of.

Our daily sex scandals are mock trials because sexual violence is a necessary part in a system that deals wrongly with sexual energies. This is the reason why negative emotions such as rage, anger and feelings of revenge will be charging the sexual urge in a way that is destructive, because this perverted drive is violent and defies any restriction. Moralism, compulsory sex morality, in this context, can by no means redirect misguided sexual energies into the right path, but in the contrary serves as a powerful social veil to make secret child and female sexual abuse even more effective and socially rampant! In last resort, every abducted, savagely raped or killed

child pays the price for the incapacity of society to integrate natural pedoemotions into its social mix.

>—Pedoemotions are temporary, transient, recurring or exclusive emosexual desires and fantasies involving children. While pedoemotions are not primarily sexual, they focus our emotional attention upon children in a way that children become more important, more attractive, more interesting to be with, more captivating and more seducing than they are for a control person with a lesser degree of pedoemotions. Pedoemotions are present in both men and women and their love objects can be either male or female children or in a bisexual form both boys and girls.

I do not talk about *statutory rape* or intercourse that is *legally deemed* as rape because done with a child, but about sadistic, violent forms of rape where the child is consciously victimized, abased and abused for the sake of abusing, and not copulated with as a partner in a mating game.

ADDRESSING THE OTHER VICTIM

This last sub-chapter addresses sexual sadists directly. It may for this reason not be of interest for the general reader on first sight; however, if you think you are *completely free* of sexual sadism you are probably wrong; we are speaking here, as I have amply pointed it out in the foregoing, about a cultural perversion, and we do not therefore need to address our individual life stories. Sadism is often hidden, don't forget that, and the higher you think you are above it, the more you are actually entangled in it! Besides that, these lines are of interest for the general reader, and also I think for law enforcement, and for people serving in education and the health care professions, for I am giving here actually a road map for developing a workable and effective therapy for sexual sadists, and this therapy, as most professionals agree, has not yet been found.

The way to heal sadism is by creating *abundant sensuality*. Sadism and sensuality are mutually exclusive. The more we are deprived of true sensuality, the more we tend to develop sadistic traits; by the same token, the more we redirect our behavior

into sensing and feeling more, and actively create more sensuality in our lives, the more we move away from sadism and again into natural and pleasurable giving-and-taking.

Or to say it bluntly, if anybody thinks he needs to rape children, the truth is that that person just needs to be *around* children.

What he really desires is the company of children, and nothing sexual in the first place.

And it's exactly because society makes it so difficult for adult males today to just be around children, to just play with them, to hug and caress them, to fondle them and cuddle with them that rape urges come up. These rape urges actually are but cries for help. They say:

—Please help me to be more around children. I can't live this way any longer. This loneliness kills me. I'm desperate. I need to get through to children.

In our subconscious mind this 'getting through to children' is understood directly and physically as a getting through into their bodies. It's as easy as that, and it's a *linguistic confusion*. Studying hypnosis has

After all, our moralistic education has prepared us well to become sexual monsters, and the fact that most of us do not really act out as sex offenders shows that we are somehow stronger than the foolish conditioning we have received and that we need to make undone as much as possible if we wish to sense and feel abundantly in relationships.

Most of us hardly ever do harm to children, which shows that we *quite effectively act counter* to the perverse conditioning we have received. The rule here may be: nature is stronger than conditioning! And nature is love, and not abasing and hurting others.

But still, the right and effective solution here would be a total change in our education of small children and the creation of a peaceful, permissive and tolerant education that respects the natural love and emotional needs of the child!

As adults we recognize our need and right for tenderness, love, sensual pleasure and sexual gratification, so why do we not grant this same right to our children?

The child needs to be *free* to exhibit his or her emotional and sexual feelings inasmuch as an adult, because this is not a question of age, but of *being human!* A human being needs to *love and copulate* as this is part of our human condition. This is not only a psychological quest, but an eminent political one, in the sense that world peace is impossible *without bringing about a fundamental change* away from moralism and toward love.

The powerless blind rage that comes up as a result of lacking autonomy is explainable as a primary infantile trauma, a feeling that has survived early childhood into adulthood; in fact it is the fear of death because in every being-in-growth there is a strong will for autonomy! It is the will to go through the growth process as fast as possible in order to become eventually like the procreators! If a child senses that their mother does not really want them to grow but remain an obedient pleasure toy and kiss puppet, and thus a partial object of the mother, the child feels threatened in their life. This fear of death is not conscious in the child but it is very present in small children who grow up with *highly narcissistic mothers,*

and it manifests as nightmares, constant bedwetting, so-called *misbehavior* and high anxiety.

Living, for a child, is synonymous with growing; hence, when growing is not allowed, living is not allowed either! Child concludes not wrongly that at the end of the day mother wants me to be dead because mother wants me to get back into the uterus and become a helpless fetus.

Why does a mother act like that, we might want to ask? Because she herself remained infantile and instead of being a mirror for her child, she only mirrors herself narcissistically.

A witch mother who asks her mirror to know if she is 'the most beautiful in the country,' as in the famous Grimm tale, has decidedly a problem with self-worth, and she has no sexual relations with men. If she had, she would get abundant feedback from men about her beauty, physical or non-physical, and she would be more self-assured and not indulge in destructive doubt.

Such a woman does not inspire much compassion, right? But imagine her as a little girl doing exactly the same, a little girl at the onset of puberty, who has got

quite a few hot regards from men already and who knows that she's at the turn into womanhood, and who is desperately curious about *how physical love might be with a man*. Would you not have deep compassion with such a little girl, would you not sadly deplore her loneliness and her lack of knowledge about physical love? And would you not join in my anger at her witch mother who deprived her since early childhood of sensuality, and destroyed her pleasure function, and this of course for selfish reasons, just as in the Grimm tale, for making a good worker out of her, a good servant, a good girl?

In my view both the witch mother and the man, have to be blamed, and certainly not the girl—and yet it's the latter way how things were handled under patriarchy since five thousand years. The big sinner was always the raped child. Fairy tales like *Little Red Riding Hood* do not talk about exotic and outlandish things but about common ones, about daily life more than anything else!

And my books take the same stance. I do not talk about remote fantasies, I am talking about *daily reality* here, and not uncommon sexual wishes! This is an etiology that today belongs to the day-to-day

practice of every psychotherapeutic cabinet, anyway when dealing with male patients.

The problem becomes more complex through the fact that the patient, as a child, could not express consciously his rage because this very idea was acting counter to the need of the child to survive in a hostile environment. As the child, especially the young child, is very dependent upon their parents, we face here always a strong denial of reality, which is the ultimate challenge in every therapy that is going to deal with rape desires.

The problem is not rage, but the fact that it was repressed since early childhood and thus acts virulently on a subconscious level, like the *Minotaur*, a fierce dragon that King Minos of Crete was holding prisoner in a tower and that, through that very imprisonment became a child-eating monster that devoured many hundreds of children once in a while when it could escape from his dungeon.

Only love can heal violent sex desires, and thus love must be promoted and lived!

Love is a highly effective alchemical process. Love means to accept one's desire unconditionally,

however violent and disruptive it may seem, and however criminal in the eyes of a stupid judgmental majority that has got no clues to heal the violent sadistic affliction that however they bring about not as an exception but as a *rule* through their complete distortion and perversion of natural child sexuality. To divide love into erotic and non-erotic love actually destroys it. All sexual monsters are highly inexperienced lovers. They have no or only a minimum of erotic knowledge and do not generally regard erotic knowledge as something worthwhile or important in life.

They are highly judgmental in their general mental setup and emotionally rather blocked. They are all but permissive. They probably do not agree with the ideas that I bring forth in this book, and in all my publications.

They do not regard child sexuality as something to be allowed, but rather something to be prohibited and harshly punished. They basically act on the lines of the mainstream fascist paradigm and have internalized the mainstream social values, and not, such as myself, alternative social values. They do not generally come out as pedophiles but rather appear

in most cases as over-adapted church goers and highly adjusted citizens. With one word, they are *false through and through* and this falseness forms part of their abject coward violence.

All love prohibitions are equally *sex prohibitions* and they do not help us cope with our more virulent energies. In the contrary, they favor child abuse and secret, domestic, hidden and coward violence acted out behind the four walls upon the socially weaker and the ultimate 'good boy' or 'good girl' who has learnt to be obedient even through the most violent, abject and humiliating treatment received, provided this treatment was inflicted by a family member and not by a so-called stranger.

Needless to add that *all this only favors abuse to be perpetuated* down the road, because the anxiety that children must cope with in this kind of climate is counter-productive to any form of healthy growth into autonomy and powerful self-reliance.

A Possible New Social Policy

On the basis of these insights we should once for all give up the taboo on child sexuality and also the taboo on consenting love and sex between children and adults not related in direct line.

The reason is that intergenerational love outside of the family really is a way out of the fusion with the matrix and all the problems it creates. Intergenerational love has an important *initiatory function* for children in their social relatedness and it represents an acceptable and constructive way to foster the *autonomy* of the child in a society that is generally against the powerful child. As such, it has an important regulatory function in modern society.

To bring this about, we have to put an end to sexual hypocrisy and accept the benefits that intergenerational love will provide in our society. Furthermore, we have to raise children in a functional, sane, healthy and permissive way so as to foster their sensuality, and we have to discard out all from of educational violence. Finally, we have to put an end to sexist ideals and raise children in an integrated way, a

way that preserves the *anima* in boys and the *animus* in girls because this will assure a lucky balance of their *yin-yang* energies.

Present mainstream education cripples the child's *emotional and sexual wholeness* and creates a high anxiety potential in our young generations. But with fear no problem can be solved and no loving world be brought about.

Worse, fear separates us from our true authentic self and brings about an authority-craving, opportunist and weak character that is prone to all kinds of manipulation and collective lies, in which ideological costume ever they come about.

If we are to survive as a human race, we have to bring about exactly the contrary character traits in our children. This is not possible without raising the emotional awareness in ourselves and them, which is for me the ultimate sociopolitical step needed in every present or future reform of our sexual laws and customs.

The problem of power and abuse, seen under this perspective, reveals to be a *secondary problem* as soul power for the naturally raised child is a

by-product of his or her autonomy. Power only becomes a problem when it is repressed, when it is thwarted. Love, too, has power, but it's not a power that degrades, abases and violates.

Thus, the problem is not power but how we handle it. Power abuse then, is not a result of power, but of the repression of power, which creates depression. The high rate of depression today in major civilizations testifies for this fact.

> —Depression affects approximately 19 million Americans, or 9.5% of the population in any given one-year period. At some point in their lives, 10% to 25% of women and 5% to 12% of men will likely become clinically depressed. It is estimated that 70% to 75% of all Americans may suffer from chronic and recurring depression, without however being clinically depressed— simply because they never consulted a doctor. In addition, suicide has been found to be a major outcome of depression. Suicide statistics in the USA show that up to 15% of those who are clinically depressed die by suicide.

It shows that most people's emotional sanity has been thwarted and that they have lost their natural soul power, and are striving to gain more secondary powers in form of social status, material possessions, and dominance over others.

Once you understand *that*, you understand all. Life itself is power. Nature is powerful. It cannot only create, but also destroy its very creation. Think only of an earthquake!

While we might not be able to ultimately control the power of nature, we can positively influence it, as the sages of old taught us, by handling our own human power responsibly.

Chapter Six

Six Steps for Changing Your Emotional Reality

＊

Introduction

A very effective way, among others, to heal a sadistic affliction is to change your self-image. This is an evolutionary consciousness process you can trigger by yourself, and without going through a whole complex cycle of inner healing of your early imprints.

These imprints will then be dissolved by your own emonic flow, directed by your consciousness. I see this as a *6-Step* Process:

▸ 1) Acceptance;

▸ 2) Realizing Your Love;

▸ 3) Facing Your Now;

- ▸ 4) Making a Value Decision;

- ▸ 5) Taking Action;

- ▸ 6) Affirming Your Identity

Human behavior cannot be rammed into people; only on the basis of acceptance, behavior can be changed on a long-term basis.

Without seeing *what is*, you cannot progress, and will eternally be stuck in your moralistic split existence that makes you deny the very reality of suffering and its cause.

As long as you stay with the inner dichotomy, the schizophrenic split of life in *should be behavior* and *real behavior*, you will be torn up in guilt and fear and change will be blocked.

As paradoxical as this sounds, what is needed before change can occur is that you see the value in *immorality* or non-morality, and the destructiveness of all morality. Liberated from the burden of moralistic trash in your mind and soul, you are able to look at the magic mirror of your own mind, and without beautifying anything you see there.

This really means you face yourself with all your pain, your suffering, your affliction, your perverse needs and desires, your need for violence, your conscious or unconscious fear of *free emotional flow* and how you block the self-regulatory processes of your organism, which is ultimately the reason that you perpetuate the very problem or hangup that stands in the way of your evolution.

So you look at yourself really through the mirror of your own conscious mind. And the miracle is that the pattern will change through this very regard, once you put your full emotional flow into this internal focus, into this introspection of your inner landscape, facing your shadow without wavering.

Only on the basis of freedom true growth is thinkable and as long as you deny this freedom, the choice namely that you have *to choose evil*, you will remain a slave of your inner complexes and the fatality of your conditioning. Only if you are able to consciously choose evil because you are free of the total falseness of so-called morality, you will be able to choose good!

Prior to even starting the work, it is necessary that you let go of the dualism so ingrained in Western

history and philosophy, because it splits you in a weak-flesh person and a should-be person, a *real person* and a *fake person*, as it splits actions in 'good' ones and 'bad' ones, as it splits emotions in 'acceptable' ones and 'unacceptable' ones.

As long as you are fragmented, as long as you have split your worldview in a (rough) real world and an (ideal) should-be world, no healing can be achieved, as real healing always is an experience of gained or regained *wholeness*.

So long as you are on the moralistic track, you cannot be healed of sadism, because it's *moralism* that brought about your sadistic affliction, in the first place. The Bible formulates this wisely in the catchy formula 'Don't judge lest ye be judged.' Yet it has to be seen that as a sadist, you are a moralist, a judger of the first order, and most often also a hair-splitter and pharisaic who speaks with 'two tongues' and whose morality is not an authentic but a false 'double' morality. So the choice is one of 'Love or Morality?' prior to even starting to dream about healing an affliction that really is no child play, which is after all why our psychiatric establishment still believes it is incurable.

So when you are ready to start, after letting go of *false morality* which is the shield behind you hide your real self, you can begin the work.

The first thing you need to do is just facing your now, your emotional reality. While it may be painful to really look at it without shying away from acknowledging all the ugly details, this first regard is really important, while it may be shocking. It means you have to strip yourself naked in front of yourself, really letting go of your false securities and all the bunch of lies you have made up to justify your sadistic longings, which bring real harm to others and to yourself. But here is where *acceptance* comes in, for when you do this, you need to do it in a mood of compassion, not in a mood of accusation. You are not here to judge yourself, as this is as bad and dysfunctional as judging others.

As a first step in your 6-Steps self-therapy plan, you may experience it as extremely difficult to accept yourself as you are, including your sadistic desires, whatever they are like, but it's really the starting point of your healing process to be set in place. This is simply so because when you remain judging yourself, you remain split in two, and thus fragmented, while

when you accept yourself, you have mastered the first hurdle on your way to become whole, and integrated.

Acceptance is also the way of getting rid of your accumulated guilt and shame, and believe me, there is no sadist who is not silently his worst judge and thereby puts an incredible amount of guilt and shame upon himself or herself. Guilt and shame however are toxic, really, in that they not only tear down the real self and replace it by a mask-like inauthentic fake self, but they also lead to psychosomatic disease and can even make for cancer or immune insufficiency syndrome later on in life, if the affliction was not tackled by therapy.

The second important step is to realize that, for example if you love children, your sadistic desires regarding children are not the outflow of your love, but of the very *repression* of your love. So to return to normal, you need to realize your original love for children, without judging it, and despite the fact that the largely ignorant meta group judges and condemns it. But you are the lover, not they, so you need to know better, and you have the responsibility to *live your love*, if ever, constructively without inflicting harm on another, adult or child. Which

means in many cases that you live your love with the utmost caution and often also platonically, namely when sexual activity would bring danger to the child and yourself, because the consequences of discovery would be devastating.

But you will realize that even when you live your love platonically, the very fact that you are around your preferred love object most of the time makes for healing about eighty percent of your sadistic longings—which will simply vanish off. To repeat it, these longings are the result of non-acceptance and because you are *starving emotionally* when you deny your most vital love desires *in origo*.

When you do this, you are facing your now, and also the societal situation of your love, which in case of *pedophilia* really is not a nice situation, neither for the lovers nor the children who dare to engage in those uncoded relations that our present society treats in very similar ways as it treated alternative medicine, alchemy, abortion or sorcery back in the Middle-Ages. And for those who ignore it, I may note here that childlove was well part of the knowledge taboo the Church enforced by means of the *Inquisition*, for consensual love with children was

indeed what enlightened and educated people such as noble men, professors, healers, alchemists and astrologers were not shying away from, in those times (while these details were carefully traced out from our history books).

They knew, as today the *pedophiles*, or most of them, that consensual love cannot be a crime, as love generally cannot be a crime in the case the relationship is consensual, while our society uses a rhetoric very similar to the *Inquisition* to condemn, ban and demonize those relationships.

In fact, it's more than a mere rhetoric, it's a systematic and absolutely undemocratic propaganda that is very little rational and pervaded by myths.

To stay untouched by these lies and half-truths, as a lover, is certainly not easy. I would say it's not unlike walking on a rope several hundred meters off the ground, like an acrobat, but that is love.

Sorry, if this sounds disturbing to you, but love was never and is never easy, among adults neither. It's a comforting belief to think that adult-adult love relations were free of stress and fears, while in truth, there is not much of a difference. In all love, courage

is needed, and be it the most platonic and altruistic love there is. Mother Theresa needed an almost superhuman courage to carry out her work before she was famous and acclaimed, for what she did went against all established morality, in the countries where she practiced her charities. Hence the need to make a *value decision*, and stick to it, which means to stay true to your soul values, without bothering too much of the social values in place that may contradict them.

The next step, then, is to simply take action, instead of sitting home and throwing one depression after the other, or becoming an alcoholic or drug addict. This means you need to affirm your emotional identity which is the real power of your total being.

Facing Your Emotional Reality

Your inner shadow or demon, as a major instance within your inner selves, which embodies the retrograde vital flow, will only collaborate in your healing and let you free *if you let him free in the first place*, and stop judging and condemning him with your shallow good-bad distinctions that have

absolutely no value and no validity in real life. Your Sunday school opinions are valid for *Kindergarten*, but this is real life, and if you don't see that you will remain forever a 'good boy' or a 'good girl' to your mom but not a full, mature and responsible human.

I have had in my free support service several of those hopeless young men who are eternally brave, nice and helpful, while they are torn up inside by the most urgent, violent and difficult-to-handle sexual needs, but in most cases several years of daily support and advice could not help them change simply because they regularly refuse to *leave* their emotionally abusive mothers and remain caught in their non-liquidated Oedipus Complex, thus perpetuating the fatal codependence they lived with their mothers through their younger years.

And while there are opportunities for them all the time for leaving their fatally dangerous situation by moving to another town or by accepting work abroad, or simply by taking a room for themselves instead of sharing the flat with their mothers, they tend to not even take the first step to reach out into autonomy and to begin living their own lives.

Typically, these men received a highly restrictive religious education that stiffened their healthy inner selves by hypertrophying their *inner controller*, and bringing their whole inner setup out of balance.

I also observed that these men are highly imitative, very little original, and intellectually rather mediocre in their overall mental penetration and performance, and this lack of brilliance can well be the outcome of their lacking emotional flow and the fear barrier that acts like a magic wand between their desires and the fulfillment of these desires.

In such a case, all support is vain as the very initiative for healing their affliction is lacking with these men. I even came to think that free support is actually a bad idea, which is why I stopped it recently. It's really a further handicap to their morbid fatalism and persistent lack of action for bringing about a change in their inner setup and outer behavior. For they know there is no free lunch, thus at least unconsciously, they know that free coaching cannot have 'real value' in a society where 'do ut des' is the established order.

I don't want to get on a tangent here, but I think I should mention what the trigger was for me to

understand that free coaching is a big mistake. It was Reiki that got me to this insight. In Reiki, the healing system founded by the Japanese natural healer *Usui*, it is recognized that healing is effected by a specific organismic energy that the Japanese call 'intelligent energy' (rei-ki in Japanese, where 'rei' means intelligent and 'ki' means vital energy).

That is why for obtaining one of the three Reiki healer degrees, a financial compensation must be paid to the instructor, which has been set in precise terms by Usui. For example for the 3rd degree, Reiki Master, the internationally recognized compensation is $20,000, and this is so wherever the degree is being taken. The reason for remuneration is that money is equally an energy, while materially speaking it seems to be just paper that is given a 'value' by the banking systems around the world.

But on the spiritual level, this is different for on this level money is an energy. Hence the idea to give a certain amount of energy for receiving a certain amount of (healing) energy.

This is so for obtaining the degree as it is true for actually receiving a Reiki treatment.

And that's the simple reason why Reiki healers nowhere in the world give free treatments! Think about that, and you may understand why I imperatively had to end free coaching, for it leads to the person to being coached to develop into a social parasite!

Ultimately, and besides these considerations, I have a feeling that these kind of men will have to choose evil once in their lives and *commit a terrible act* in order to wake up from their stiffening mediocrity, and get on the path of healing and real life, leaving their shell existences behind forever.

Even before I became a coach and corporate trainer, during my former career as a lawyer, I have seen many such cases that I would not like to divulge here, so much the more as the mass media are today indulging in publicizing almost daily about this kind of horror crimes. But the public ignores the true and long-term causes that drive men to the point to set an act of horror in order to initiate their process of self-healing.

While it's so much easier to undo the knot of codependence without using the Damocles sword,

this is the kind of choices every human must make for himself or herself.

My ultimate motivation, then, to work as a coach came initially from such kind of crimes, because there was a moment when as a young law student I said to myself:

—It's futile to study law, as law itself is futile. People will only live lawful lives if they are not in an inner prison that one day explodes, because nobody can live without freedom. So what we need is not law, but freedom, and as I see that all those who commit crimes are caught in a fatal state of inner bondage to their urgent needs, desires and inner wounds and conflicts, what I have to do in order to help is to directly get in touch with these people and offer my support to them.

That is why, as a result of this profound insight, I changed my professional career after finalizing my law doctorate and became a coach and training facilitator.

If you have the courage to initiate the first decisive step, the energy will follow and you will see that every next sprocket in the chain reaction of your liberation will be easier than the previous one.

When you can get to a point to view your affliction as a *state of bondage,* you will get a feel what I mean by liberation, and you will see that this is a *process,* not just a magic stroke that will change you from devil to angel. You are *not* a devil and you will *not* become an angel. Both devils and angels are inferior to human beings, because they cannot choose. They are destined to be either devils or angels, to either do bad or good, while the genius of the human being is the capacity to be both, and much more.

TRIGGERING SELF-AWARENESS

To initiate this process, we look at what *is* and not at what *should be.* If we see what is, we can as a result see why it is as it is. If we ask what should be, we build an ideal that is different from the reality we are in, and we split ourselves in two: an observer and a dreamer. The *observer* sees what is, the *dreamer* longs for what should be. The first is a *realist,* the second an *ideologist.* We will see ourselves in conflict soon since every decision we take will look different if we see it either from the realist's side or from the ideologist's

side. This is the basic schizoid split most people suffer from who are reared with a moralistic or idealistic educational paradigm. They can never be sure what really they hold true since they are, so to say, caught in two truths. And that is why they speak with two tongues. They tend to argue in ways like 'Man is bad but God wants us to be good' or 'People are rude by nature but if they join the Communist Party they turn to be caring people' or 'People are uneducated and bad but our Great Theosophy renders them enlightened and good.'

All this is pure schizophrenia and shows the basic split humanity is suffering from since the moralistic worldview prevails, and this is at least since written history exists.

To become whole requires us to acknowledge this split and to face our sadistic drives and desires, our need to compensate for all the hurt we have suffered in early childhood. It requires us to face our inner wounds and become vulnerable again for feeling-with, for compassion, and thus develop empathy.

The next step, then, is to become aware where our need for violence is rooted in. When we observe our

pleasure function, we see that the repression of pleasure more or less automatically creates violence. Violence, then, is a *negative pleasure function* in the sense that it comes about when pleasure is repressed.

Our early need for body pleasure was denied to us to a large extent. Most of us, in childhood and youth, have been withheld from engaging in erotic play, and even more so have we been denied free sexual relations with other children or adults. Instead, we perceived sexuality as *the big taboo* and the activity that is most dangerous to engage in while our bodies strongly asked for sex.

Society made us believe that sexuality is bad while violence is good and thus conditioned us from childhood to accept violence as an *ersatz* for the lost paradise of body pleasure. In fact, society stole us our bodies during childhood, depriving us of the intrinsic feeling to *own* them, namely by having the autonomy to *use* them.

Once you are able to see this, you will understand how definite and fatal the consequences are of repressing children's natural need for body pleasure. Then, and only then will you be ready to gain real

insight into the precise mechanisms that perpetuate violence.

You will then be able to see that the physical punishment of children is one of the pillars of handing down the murder culture from one generation to the next, thus perpetuating violence in time and space. You will then also comprehend the link between the repression of emotions and the upsurge of perversion as a secondary drive structure—while the unbent human nature in children is not perverse, and not pervertible. And to repeat it, Sigmund Freud's assumption of the 'polymorphously perverse infant' is a myth, and perhaps the most cynical projection ever done by a human male upon infants.

In a way, Freud betrayed his abhorrent confusion between sensuality and sexuality. An infant indeed is totally sensual, and for good reason, simply because the five senses are much sharper, much more refined in the infant than in the human adult.

The distortion of perception that goes along with thwarting natural emotions in early childhood is the key for understanding why humans can be bought into denying themselves the most basic of fulfillment there is in life: love.

And it is because we ourselves were deprived in the first place of the freedom to develop our full emotionality in childhood that we deny it to our children and instead instill in them fear, suspicion and violence. If we looked at things with an innocent eye and without any compulsive morality paradigm, we would naturally perceive that children are emotionally much more balanced than we adults are.

Naturally raised children are not only not sadistic, they are also, what counts even more, *sexually* not sadistic and thus achieve sexual fulfillment without threat and without violence.

Most of us have never known such kind of children since we ourselves grew up in a repressive environment and our peers suffered from the same cruel prohibitions, and sadism, especially in school, was rampant.

But whoever had the opportunity to meet so-called *wild children* knows that they are much more caring, empathic, flexible and intelligent than children raised within the repressive paradigm.

My extensive research on permissive education has shown me in addition that these children also

tend to be healthier, more flexibly and emotionally intelligent, more responsible and more practical than children raised within the authoritarian educational system.

I will now comment on every of the six steps, and you should read this in one row, from the first to the last step, because there is an order in this sequence.

1) Practicing Acceptance

The first important step you must take for the realization of emotional reflow and the dissolution of sadism is acceptance of your love and desire, and a clear decision to not repress it. Repression does not lead anywhere. It is a way of going around a problem, not a way of solving it.

Whatever your emotional and randomly sexual longings are, stay with them and do not deny them. Instead, try to get away from all and every label that you see society attaches to your particular attraction and try to see the real beauty of your love.

For example, if you feel special about togetherness with children and have a strong emotional predilection for them, you may want to

study how attraction toward children has been faced
and lived in the Greek and Roman Empires, during
Antiquity, and later on during Christianity and the
Victorian Era, until our modern times.

> —I have conducted such research; it shows
> the constancy of adult-child sexual
> interaction as a matter of cultural choice.
> However, if this choice could be in any way
> in accordance with 'morality' is not a
> question I am asking, and for good reason.
> In fact, the two modes of argumentation are
> irreconcilable; either one is able to see the
> facts of life, or one has been rendered blind
> to them by a moralistic roof structure that
> distorts perception.

When you are able to stay away from overly
negative voices, you will see clearly how misinformed
most people are about these matters and how fanatic,
and how far from the reality of children's emotional
life.

You will then eventually understand that most
people who pretend to know about this subject do
actually know *nothing* about it. And that, while they
think they act in the child's best by prohibiting
children to really live their lives and loves, they are

talking over the head of children, instead of talking *with* children, and inquiring what children really want. And then you will perhaps realize that most of your knowledge is taken from books and lifeless reports, and based upon so-called authorities; and that you do not have any living experience with erotically loving children and thus are *disqualified from the start* from participating in any form of discussion of the problem.

Instead of listening to these negative voices, you may then begin to strengthen your own inner positive voices regarding emotions, love and sexuality. Only *you* can be your advocate, once you are ready for it, once you have stopped being your own judge.

Judging yourself is the worst you can do. It means you are falling in the moralistic trap, which really serves nobody. Instead, try to be every day a little more tolerant with yourself, a little more permissive, a little more understanding.

When you stop considering your own attractions, and those of others, as an affliction, and begin to see everybody's emotional predilections as a gift, as a blessing, you start out to see the uniqueness in yourself and other humans—instead of being

intimidated by the idiotic standards imposed by a violent and ignorant society.

Giving up repressing desires also means to inquire in the messages we receive through dreams, from the unconscious realm. We do not always understand those messages, and perhaps not all dreams are messages.

Dreams are certainly also destined to help us digest events, to overcome deep hurt and thus to favor inner healing as well as preparing and fostering change.

The beneficial effects of regularly monitoring your dreams do not require you to understand their meaning! It is enough noting your dreams in a booklet, every morning, right after waking up, and from time to time reading through this booklet.

Consider it as a collection of personal stories, dream stories, and read them with delight. Even though some of them may be appalling because of frightening animals appearing, strange things happening or violence becoming staged, they represent an accurate reflection of your inner

thoughts, your inner reality, and as such have to be taken serious.

And they are creative productions of our mind, and the language they speak is a part of our own symbolic language.

Furthermore, dreams tell us at times things that we never admitted to ourselves or that we always ignored. They reveal a part of our truth. By integrating the messages of our dreams, our thinking becomes more holistic, and less fragmented; as a result, our actions will be more authentic. You will also see that dreams reveal to you how secure or insecure you are with regard to your love choices.

Do you accept your love? Or do you fight it? Do you try to go around it or cover it up? Do you distract yourself in order not to think about it?

All these questions are reflected upon in your dreams, and the answers you get from them may be confused or clear.

When I am confused, my dreams will show confusion while when my choices are clear, I will have clear and straightforward dreams.

You may wonder why you should at all get this feedback from your dreams? I do not say that you cannot do without it, but it surely is one important tool for getting to know yourself. It is a tool among others. If you do not feel like exploring into your dream world, you do not have to. But it is certainly true that you can advance faster in the realization of your goals when you really know what you want.

Life is responsive. It guides us through constant feedback, it helps us to know ourselves, and this, as I said, not only in dreams but also in daily life. But this feedback depends also on our clarity of mind, or more precisely put, on the clarity of our wishes.

If your desires are confused and mixed with guilt and shame, there is a chance that you will find this very confusion in your mind reflected in the outside world, and you will build this confusion into your relationships, which is the deeper meaning behind triangular relations. If you are not sure what you want and should want, you will get both, but in a way that is problematic.

2) REALIZING YOUR LOVE

Once you have learnt to practice *Life Authoring*, you can begin authoring not only your life, but also your love and thereby gain clarity about your love choices, about your emotional predilections.

I would like to stress at this point that one possible etiology of sadism are repressed homoerotic wishes that, instead of being joyfully admitted and embraced, became charged with fear and disgust.

Let me give an example. When I want to punish women by acting out sadistically on females, by raping them, what my behavior expresses is *anger*, and not love; then I rather *reject* women instead of embracing them.

This anger may be a result of my *unconscious homoerotic desires,* and it may dissolve once I give green light for engaging in a same-sex adventure. What I am saying is that homoerotic wishes are a natural add-on to our sexual completeness, without for that reason rendering us 'a homosexual' or 'a lesbian' in the sense these terms are used today in modern society.

My research brought to daylight that these emotional predilections for partners of the same sex are most of the time *transitory* and mark certain phases or periods in our lives. They are for most people not a fixated sexual condition, and thereby are not either-or choices. It may be like in the *yin-yang* energetic formula. In the black circle that represents *yin* energy, there is a small white circle that stands for the growing part of *yang* within the overwhelming part of *yin*. This small white circle will thus grow until it is as large as formerly was the black circle while the black circle will diminish to a smaller size and reside in the large white circle.

Thus what we have here is not a static idea, but a living dynamic movement, a steady transformation. *Yin* plus a little *yang* inside transforms into *yang* plus a little *yin* inside and back again. What this means, translated into less abstract terms, is that every man once in a while becomes woman and every woman once in a while becomes man.

When you are a man, why are you at pains admitting that you are composed not only of male but also of female characteristics and that, as a result you are actually a mix between male and female

ingredients? In your individual *emotional identity code* is contained also an information to what extent you are *yang* and to what extent you are *yin*.

By the way, you can look this up using astrology and numerology. For example in my astrological chart I saw with some surprise that my own mix, while I am a man, is composed of 55% *yin* and 45% *yang*, which means that in terms of my unique emotional ID tag, I am predominantly *yin* or female.

Thus, at the start of your finding out about yourself, and inquiring in the roots of your sadistic desires, you should check in which way you may be locked into rejecting certain sexual fantasies and experiences. Use your fantasy for this inquiry, let your imagination grow wild and see what happens in the little films that you make up in your mind.

I have myself never repressed my bisexuality, and I know that this sexual arousal that many men so vehemently deny when it goes to sexual mating with a partner of equal gender and age can come about. It comes about not spontaneously in many cases, that is true, but as a possible result of deep affection and the voluntary giving-up of any idea of machismo, domination, control and moralistic righteousness. It

can come about when two men or women share a deep friendship. It may come about. Or it may not. I am speaking about an *option*. I do not say that all people should have sex with their friends. We are not talking here about what we ought to do, but what we possibly wish to do and can do if we wish it and as long as we wish it. I am talking about affection and sexual options. I am saying that it is silly to exclude per se any possibility of sex with a partner of the same sex. Nature has not written anywhere that we are locked in heterosexual behavior. On the other hand, it would be silly to force ourselves onto any kind of fashionable concept of bisexuality if we really cannot get along with the idea.

What I am saying is that you should *check it out for yourself* where you possibly and unconsciously have violated your own nature somewhere, somehow, in the past, as a youngster obeying to conditioning rules, or by conditioning yourself to what seemed to be 'acceptable behavior.'

Put away this self-imposed restriction and liberate yourself from the energetic constriction that goes along with it. *There is no acceptable behavior.* Period. When you start from here, you will see that you begin

to feel that there are indeed more options for attaining emotional and sexual wholeness than you might have thought.

And when you start thinking on these lines, on the lines of pleasure, namely, your sadism will automatically go down the river! This is so because sadism is anti-pleasure, sadism is a form of distorted thinking on the lines of coercion, like society does, like the law does, like most religions do. *Sadism is conditioned behavior.* Pleasure-seeking, however, is natural behavior. That is the difference.

Again, to be very clear: you should *not force* any change in behavior; you should not apply a paradigm to your life that you find not fitting for yourself. But you can ask that question to yourself, that question where you might be blocked or locked into something that is not your total being, your original being. Once you have done that and asked that question, you simply stay with the question.

What does that mean? It means you stay with that question without searching for an answer. The answer will come when you have forgotten about the question, and in ways that may surprise you. The answer will come, to be sure, but only once you have

built enough *emotional awareness*; you will be able to link the answer back to the question you have asked.

For most people, the answer will come in a way that is so subtle that in that moment, they don't remember the question and thus do not know how, in the first place, they have made a quantum jump on their evolutionary scale. But never mind, in both ways, there is evolution, and it doesn't matter if you are aware of it at first, or not.

3) Facing Your Now

It is important for progressing to first see where we are! You cannot start from point zero, but always have done some part of the way before. Thus you should see where you are *now* and what the way is you already have done.

Only by facing your present situation, by assessing your present state of being, you can make a true evolution. It is essential that you face your present business, even though it might be very depressing to look at it. Your present situation is the outcome of your past thoughts! So don't be surprised if it looks negative, shabby, ugly and hopeless.

Simply acknowledge that your previous thought patterns were negative, shabby, ugly and hopeless, and that it is for that reason logical that your present situation is reflecting this negative pattern.

Facing your situation does not mean that you should be fatalistic and focus upon the negative points in your life. It only means to face what *is*.

Once you see what your present situation is like, in its totality, you can peacefully acknowledge that you have been on the wrong track before and you can correct the thought patterns and the emotional patterns that led to producing negative results.

It's like an entrepreneur who assesses his present state of business, who has suffered losses and now gets to find out the exact reasons for those losses, so that he can learn from his mistake and correct his previous action, and do it better in the future.

Sometimes you need to get a little distance to your present struggle. You might be in an emotionally difficult situation where it is hard to have a cool head, and you might want to do some relaxation or meditation or just become quiet inside in order to focus on your energy. Avoid distractions, cinema or

television since this surely does not favor introspection but will distort your inner visions.

First of all, it is important that you believe in yourself and the truth of your inner visions! Those visions, what you see or feel when you are relaxed and centered, those ideas that come up and that may seem crazy to you at first, are part of your innermost truth. Thus, they are important messages from your inner world, and they have value for guiding you toward a better, more complete reality, a reality in which you realize your love constructively, without the compulsive need to coerce somebody into being a passive dummy for your sexual abreaction.

Facing your situation also means to see yourself for a moment from the vantage point of some sort of observer, somebody who is impartial, who does not take sides, who does not judge, but who has empathy for you. You have this observer within you and need only activate it in order to profit from the insights it can deliver. But for this to happen you need to be fully relaxed. This inner observer is most of the time dysfunctional because of a dominant inner critic.

The inner critic is the instance in you that judges yourself, that always knows everything better, that is

haughty and arrogant and that tells you something like 'You're a little piece of shit, so why do you bother to improve yourself? You can never do anything valuable, so better you act out like mad or just kill yourself right away!'

It is fatal to listen to the voice of the inner critic; it may be the fact that you do listen to it why you cannot manage your life properly and run amok once in a while.

I believe that indeed the main reason why passion crimes are committed is that this inner critic is too strong and does not allow these individuals to admit their vulnerability, and does therefore not allow them to realize their desire in any natural way because of a moralistic denial.

To break the *cycle of sexual violence* is possible once you get to allowing yourself sexual pleasure in a natural, shared and sociable way, by making friends, following basic customs to socialize, building trust and long-lasting relationships and experience sexual love on a mutually consenting basis.

4) MAKING A VALUE DECISION

Sometimes it is necessary to have the courage for opposing society and its nonsensical sex laws in order to live your desire in a constructive way. The important thing is that you comply with cosmic law by restraining from inflicting suffering on any other creature.

The laws on earth are very volatile and they are often not in accordance with eternal spiritual laws. They actually vary from country to country and from epoch to epoch.

If you comply with all of the ideological and economic values that go along with our morality code, you will become a total conformist. Then you may foolishly pride yourself in having bent your inner nature to the breaking point, and have got to the opposite of what is natural. *And then you may not wonder that you become violent as a beast!*

If you still struggle with these values, if you allow them to be valid for you, you will be in trouble, you will be confused, since they do not go along with your inner nature, but rather oppose it.

Thus you must make a clear *value decision*. What are the values that count for you, and which ones do not count for you?

If you are not clear about those questions you cannot focus upon your own position regarding your love because you will find yourself in a value conflict.

A value conflict is a situation where you are not sure which values count for you and are valid for your life, other people's or the majority's values, or your own values?

While it is true that only your own values can have an impact on your life, this is not as obvious as it seems on first sight. Many people actually share the values of others without being aware that these values do not fit or fit only partially their own lives.

That means that they more or less imitate other peoples' lifestyles without being aware that such behavior deprives them of their own truth—and of their soul power!

Your sense of intuition may not be well developed and you might need to trust yourself more in order to be able to delve into this reservoir of information

readily available to you. You can enhance your inner clarity by doing the following:

▸   Imagine what you most would like to do now;

▸   Get to write down a wish list, that is, a list all your wishes;

▸   Find out what the ultimate priority is for you in life.

When you do these activities, your intuition and not your intellect will speak.

In order for this to happen and for facilitating this process, do away with thinking in opposites. Instead, focus on what you wish to realize. Opposites trap you in that they split you into positive and negative parts, the positive parts affirming our desire, the negative parts denying or contradicting it.

When you are split in opposites you are less powerful and your clarity about your goals is veiled by fear and indecisiveness.

When you make the wish list, do not ask if those wishes are in reach or not, depending on your financials and your present circumstances. Doing so will defeat you! Be a little childish and just put down

your wishes; put them on paper, fixate them. And say Yes to them! So write them down without thinking, as a quite mechanical activity, just to spit it out, to get it done, to have it on paper.

While you do that, nod! That's how your body participates in the process and your body cannot lie. Your body is always honest. Nodding your head says: 'Yes, I stand behind those wishes. They are what I truly need and want in life, period.'

In this first draft, do not give a priority to your wishes nor any order. Just note them. Once you have a page filled with wishes, then, a few days later, and with a fresh mind, put an order and priorities to your wishes. You may then realize that some wishes are more important to you than some others.

Then detect one wish you consider more important than all the others and get clarity why this wish gets on top of your priority list. Then write it on top of your new wish list, the new list that classifies your wishes, and puts priorities.

This is certainly a challenge, but it is not more of a challenge as any of the great challenges we are

familiar with from the autobiographies of famous people. *You will be a hero.*

A hero is simply one who is able to realize a unique mission and to work with spiritual power for this purpose.

A hero, you may ask? But that's for the movies, right?

Yes and no. It's for the movies, certainly, but it's also for real life.

Have you never met a person that you thought truly is a hero or heroine? A hero is not what you see in the false world of television every day; it is not the fighter for righteousness and justice, and similar myths that are set in place for the moral conditioning of the masses. A hero is simply the fighter for a unique individual mission. A hero is a person who responds positively to the challenge of saying *Yes* to their own desire—whatever it happens to be. In the wistful words of Joseph Campbell, the great mythologist, a hero follows *his call.*

When you do this and use spiritual powers to accomplish your mission while being confident that the universe will provide you with exactly what you

need, you will end up being powerful and happy, and you will not infringe eternal laws.

5) Taking Action

You can't remain eternally stagnant, thinking about options, without putting a decisive step toward realization. You must take action!

Evaluate all the options you have. Make an option catalogue; then visualize every one of these options, as if seeing yourself as the actor in a film that plays a version of that option.

While you see this film in your mental eye, be as relaxed as possible. If you feel fear coming up, stop the session and begin it anew in a moment you are more relaxed and more positive.

Do this little game with every option in your catalogue. Then evaluate every single option as to its effectiveness to bring you closer to your desired goal.

Finally, decide which option you like most and focus upon it so as to find out what exactly you need to do in order to bring about this event. Ask yourself:

▸   What is the action I need to take first?

▸   What are the obstacles? Can they be removed, and how?

▸   What are the risks? Can they be kept at stake?

▸   What is the ultimate advantage from realizing this option?

If you are clear about every step to take, go out and make it happen. Be always watchful, but trust the goodness of your fate. Don't be overcautious and coward, but do on the other hand do not take *unnecessary* risks.

And firmly believe in that destiny helps you to realize your love without hurting other humans! Trust that your love will be realized without hurting those you love and who love you.

I think that all great people once came upon their own way and set out to live it in a focused and strongly personal manner.

Frank Sinatra sings 'My Way' and his life showed that indeed he had unusual powers, on one hand, and an undeniable shadow, on the other.

Our shadow is what gives depth to the picture, it is our hidden power, our reservoir of energy to be put to

good use. Our shadow is our chance to become true individuals and to live original, authentic lives, without the need to imitate others.

Only by becoming very sensitive to others, we can heal the sadistic affliction. This sensitivity can be built in various ways. Let me suggest a few that I have tried out and that worked:

- ▸ Reduce alcohol consumption to a strict minimum;

- ▸ Reduce smoking to a strict minimum;

- ▸ Reduce eating red meat to a strict minimum;

- ▸ Try to live a simple lifestyle and avoid large festivities;

- ▸ Avoid to aggrandize yourself in your fantasies.

Is this society one day mature enough to face that love is love, and as such, as love, is not subject of power abuse, and that love is part of the human karma, the total human experience? And will they eventually be able to admit this fact without being afraid of this or that sexual act? To get there means to overcome the manipulation of all religions, violent

state doctrines and power ideologies of all times and once for all *to attain freedom.*

Then only, and not before, will there be responsible social mores and rules. To speak with Krishnamurti, instead of thinking, reasoning and arguing in our mind, you should try to develop *complete attention* so that you intuitively grasp the whole of the question.

This *watchful passive attention,* when focused inside and upon our longings and desires is *erotic intelligence.* It reflects the deep truth that our body and our emotions have their own intrinsic intelligence—that may well differ from the voice of our mind. Erotic intelligence is a natural outflow of consciousness, of acute awareness.

However, unfortunately, emotional and erotic consciousness is *underdeveloped* in our culture.

Once you see why society fights paraphilias as the ultimate monstermind software in the human setup, you must come to understand the psychological mechanism of *projection.*

With other words, you must come to the point to see the fact that society always projects on certain

people or groups the content of consciousness that it has blinded out from its official dogma of reality.

What my mind cannot assimilate, it projects upon others, a group, a lifestyle, a condition, or a race. In order to hide from myself the fact that *I am violent*, I will develop and display a zeal for fighting violence in the world.

Instead of tackling the problem where it really is, within myself, I try to solve it on a fantasy stage: the level of 'humanity.'

If the many abuse victims that go around making the world save for universal love *could see how abusive they are with their own children*, they would probably end up totally depressed—but that would be to their best, for they would probably stop that zealous fight that is but a blind man's buff.

Hiding desires brings about dishonesty and myths. One of them is the myth that there was something like *sexual purity*. It's a word that is to be found in the spiritual literature all over the world.

While purity is certainly a quality to be appreciated in any human being, sexual purity as a virtue is entirely different of what the mass public tends to understand

under this word; it does certainly *not mean* emotional numbness.

True purity is virtue and embraces truthfulness, honesty, integrity and straightforwardness. It is quite the contrary of the *false, hypocrite and perversely dishonest* attitude to be found in circles close to churches regarding the reality of our emotions and sexual feelings.

The majority's response to their own natural emotions is but repression and oblivion, the classical attitude of the cannot-be-what-must-not-be that we know from Goethe's *Faust*. They are *afraid* of erotic novelty, and tend to fight any form of erotic awareness that would bring about erotic intelligence.

They try to handle life not by intelligent understanding but by adapting to strict dogmatic rules, in one word: they are not humans, but dummies.

The consequences are communication disabilities and an appalling lack of creativeness in the common man or woman.

These are not just minor problems in today's modern consumer cultures, and they are not just

random appearances; in fact, they make out a great part of the work of psychologists and therapists. Creativity can hardly develop in a climate of suspicion and emotional repression. It depends on qualities like *spontaneity, trust, openness, honesty* and *straightforwardness.*

Energetically speaking, this is well explainable by the higher bioplasmatic vibration of truly creative people.

People who are not fragmented are charismatic. Their *e-force*, their vital energy is felt as inspiring and they easily respond to it by enthusiasm and a generally loving and embracing attitude that is felt as erotic so that you can experience their high magnetic charge in their presence.

That is all the secret.

Creativity can only develop within a framework of *freedom and acceptance,* and where bioenergy can freely flow—not in a nightmare of fear and persecution or, worse, *public hysteria* that is the daily reality in our paranoid culture.

Love is unity. Those who pretend that all love was per se platonic love, argue on the basis of moralistic dualism, a form of philosophical schizophrenia.

A person who enjoys vivid emotions does not need expensive medical treatments since their self-healing capacities are excellent; such a person doesn't need to use the most idiotic devices ever invented, that is, *condoms*, for they will not attract venereal disease, cancer or immune insufficiency syndrome.

An erotically satisfied person does not develop high interest in consumer goods. Their body is their primary focus when they relax and retreat from public life, and not a *gadget ersatz*, readily fabricated by modern consumer industry. Thus, erotically fulfilled people are *per se heretics* in a society that commercially exploits the repression of our primary eroticism.

6) Affirming Your Emotional Identity

The most important issue at stake behind consumerism is *identity* in the sense that the identity is typically lacking with modern citizens; that is why they are consumers in the first place, and that in turn is why they are addicted to consumption *as an ersatz* for living a meaningful life.

There is personal identity, gender identity, sexual identity, social identity, political identity, ethnic identity and national identity. Any of these identities can only grow in freedom.

That is why *child protection*, and all protection, is really counter-productive to building identity. The slave is identified as an asset of his or her master, not as a person in their own right. The modern citizen is identified as an asset of the nation state he or she belongs to, not as a person in their own right, a spiritual entity that bears a unique cosmic identity tag in form of an energy code that is written right into their vibrational field.

That is why ultimately consumer citizens do not enjoy social autonomy; they are deterred from it by a cunning and strategic denial of their soul identity.

The consumer citizen is a creature who lives with a disowned body, a body that is socially controlled and manipulated, and that is filled up with consumer goods. It's a container, a vessel for something not originally contained in it, and that is actually alien to it.

We owe this development to a very old perversion of values, namely Aristotelian dualism, which was taken over by the Church and later by the modern state, and which dissected body and soul so that the theory became possible that a person may disown her body without disowning her soul. I would go as far as saying that it was this paradigm that is at the origin of ancient and modern holocausts.

It was a common argument for missionaries for committing genocide of supposedly non-believing native populations.

They alleged that those people *did not have a soul* and were thus by definition no humans. Hitler used the same rhetoric against the Jews. This

argument is logically impossible if we hold that *body and soul are a unity* because then every creature that owns a body must own a soul. As a result, the modern citizen that lives with a disowned body equally has been deprived of their soul.

The question why modern life has no soul finds its answer here. A society of disowned individuals is a group of shadows or an ensemble of ectoplasms, but not a community of soul-beings. Tribal societies are different in their being in unity with their bodies and thus with their souls! That is why their lifestyle is filled with soul, with joy, with significance while modern society's is empty like a dried-out shell.

The only way out of consumerist projections, absurd conclusions and publicly propagated lies is *understanding*. This understanding comes about through *erotic intelligence*. It is a result of finding the answers inside, afar from political conceptions and models.

People who have problems when being in touch with their natural emotions should make serious efforts to understand and reintegrate their disowned inner selves—and the problems will disappear. Not only since Fritjof Capra's revolutionary bestseller *The*

Turning Point (1987) do we know that Darwinism is built on false premises and that the human is not a machine.

Emonics, as a science of the bioenergy, is my personal contribution to the emerging holistic social sciences that have incorporated the mind-boggling insights of quantum physics and modern systems theory. My thesis it not just an opinion, and it is neither a romantic illusion for 'bettering' sexuality.

There is nothing to better as we are perfect as humans; what is not perfect is the way we handle love, and thus the love conditions that we have set as a society, and the ways to express our human love potential. Why should I spend two decades of research for just defending an opinion? The truth is that I have nothing to defend.

We humans simply are not just 'sexual beings,' as sexology makes us believe, but we are *soul beings* first of all, and thereafter, from a psychosomatic perspective, we are *emotional plus sexual*, and thus *emosexual* beings.

This is simply so, if sexological reductionism agrees or not. Sexology does not consider emotional

preferences as factors triggering sexual attraction because emotions do not fit in their residual Darwinian scheme of 'sexual drives,' a scheme that has been taken over and reinforced by Sigmund Freud, psychoanalysis and psychological and medical practices that are mainstream today.

Mainstream social sciences see emotions only as an add-on to sexuality, as something that can be linked to sexual behavior, but not something that is genuinely involved in sexual attraction, or that even triggers sexual attraction. In fact, my hypothesis that emotional attraction is the *primal attraction* and that sexual attraction the secondary attraction, and that sexual attraction thus *follows* emotional attraction, clearly contradicts sexology.

I am aware of the fact that my hypothesis may sound queer to many psychologists and psychiatric professionals, but that is just part of the game of being a pioneer. It's here where my landscape starts and where traditional sexology ends.

It's with the term *emotional predilections* that I started my journey into a different world of cross-cultural and multi-disciplinary science that deals with some of our most important, and also of our

most controversial attractions, like human erotic attraction toward children.

From a point of view of linguistics, I share the insight Terence McKenna expressed in his book *Archaic Revival (1992),* that is, that we form reality by *forming language:*

> There are times—and this would be a great study for somebody to do—there have been periods in English when there were emotions that don't exist anymore, because the words have been lost. This is getting very close to this business of how reality is made by language. Can we recover a lost emotion by creating a word for it? There are colors that don't exist anymore because the words have been lost. I'm thinking of the word jacinth. This is a certain kind of orange. Once you know the word jacinth, you always can recognize it, but if you don't have it, all you can say is it's a little darker orange than something else. We've never tried to consciously evolve our language, we've just let it evolve, but now we have this level of awareness, and this level of cultural need where we really must plan where the new words should be generated. There are areas where words should be gotten rid of that empower political wrong thinking. The propagandists for the fascists already understand this; they understand that if you make something unsayable, you've made it unthinkable. So it doesn't plague you anymore. So planned

> evolution of language is the way to speed it
> toward expressing the frontier of
> consciousness. (Id., 214)

One reason for sexual minorities today having such a hard stand in Western society is, as McKenna suggests, the fact that not enough effort has been done from their own rings to make something sayable by having made it *thinkable*.

When I speak about *emotional awareness* as a major ingredient in holistic awareness, I impact on our reality and make it shift toward a higher level of consciousness. And doing this, I impact upon the reigning love paradigm and make it shift as well. I impact upon language because I know that this will powerfully aid the paradigm shift to happen within the next or the over next generation. Let me cite from Fritjof Capra's book *The Turning Point (1997)* to close this sub-chapter:

> These problems (…) are systemic problems,
> which means that they are closely
> interconnected and interdependent. They
> cannot be understood within the fragmented
> methodology characteristic to our academic
> disciplines and government agencies. Such an
> approach will never solve any of our difficulties
> but will merely shift them around in the
> complex web of social and ecological relations.

> A resolution can be found only if the structure of the web is changed, and this will involve profound transformations of our social institutions, values, and ideas. (Id., 6)

My systems approach to human emotions through the creation of a new terminology is a logical continuation of Capra's reasoning, extrapolated into the area of human love and sexuality.

And there is a good chance that such a new terminology will be accepted in the future, simply because it is useful.

Within the transformation we are presently going through, I believe, there is *high probability* that the values of intimacy, love and sexuality will be reconsidered, if not completely revised.

CHAPTER SEVEN

Harnessing the Power of Emotional Identity

*

THE POLITICAL ARENA

In the present last chapter I shall paint a picture how, in real life, *Emonics* can be useful as an alternative and holistic approach for comprehending the nature of sexual attraction.

My wish and desire is that this comprehensive terminology and approach for normalizing sexual paraphilias will be helpful to both the concerned, and the psychiatric profession in their role as facilitators.

The present system simply is inhuman and destructive; it shuns human dignity; it is not better than what in the darkest of ages was committed against those who were not complying with the black-coated denial dogma.

If any of our highly acclaimed psychiatrists, psychologist or psychoanalysts had a heart in their chest, they would have opened their mouth once for all to voice their concern about the systematic persecutions and the torture inflicted upon *pedophiles* by the joint-forces of government and psychiatry around the world.

They are simply system-conform agents for brainwashing the masses into consumerism and more consumerism with every year to come.

They can't be trusted for they have not set any signal that they have reached a state of emotional maturity, and professional autonomy that sets them apart from the grinding state machineries in their destructive stupidity. If they had, the situation wouldn't be as it is, today, and I wouldn't have written this book.

This does not mean that I am against psychiatry; not at all. I had tremendous help in my life through a psychotherapy done with a wistful psychiatrist who was really the exception that proves the rule.

If I had no hope in the psychiatric profession, I wouldn't have drafted a legal bill that actually

empowers psychiatric facilitators and gives them the responsibility that our police forces simply cannot bear.

The problem is not psychiatry, but the fact that psychiatrists do not voice their concerns, for reasons of *political correctness*, for fear of losing their reputation in a system where one tightly observes the other, and where those who are 'too alternative' are ruthlessly discarded out. To remind the reader only of Wilhelm Reich, while there are many more examples. I am not here to criticize psychiatry, but to propose the idea of empowering an independent autonomous profession of psychiatry that is acting on their own right, not as an executory agent of demonic governments.

This is, needless to add, the old ethical rule of the psychiatric profession. It is to be a facilitator for high human unfolding, and therefore, in all oppressive political systems, a force that is not 'in alignment.' To remind only that in Nazi Germany, psychiatrists who did not conform risked their lives or had to leave the country. Freud went to London, Reich to the United States, Fromm to Mexico, to name only these.

The impetus for change can only come from the political arena and it could be put in the slogan 'From Retaliation to Cooperation.' With applying a *proactive paradigm* of social interaction instead of retaliation, a system of cooperative communication with the citizen can be worked out, and entrusted expert consultants can help correct asocial and truly harmful sexual behavior.

As for now, it is certainly not reasonable and functional to found human behavior upon morality, because morality is a concept that is vague and volatile, if it's not pure fake.

There is one rule that must be firmly in place, it's that *one must not harm another*, which is, not coincidentally, the only rule of conduct obeyed by the Kahunas and other wistful native peoples, such as the Hopi, and others, around the world.

When this rule truly is respected, no government needs to fear major upheaval, nor outrageous crime incidents, as they are now the rule, because right now this rule is not respected! Why this is so is precisely because there is no real morality in our modern consumer cultures, there are no more rules and values people are living by, intuitively.

Those rules simply are dead, which is why a reformation of the whole system is an absolute necessity; and it must embrace the educational system as well, for it's there, in the cradle and the crèche, where the basic values are set for the generations to come.

With labeling people, and even children now, as 'sex offenders' or 'abusers,' nothing is achieved but a *further destruction of human potential,* and an even more global rejection of the 'positive human' who is the real human, not the 'negative human' that ghosts in the brains of our insane politicians and propagandists. The way to individual and world peace is *allowing* emotions, not repressing emotions, *allowing* sexuality, not repressing sexuality, *allowing* pleasure, not frowning upon pleasure, *allowing* new forms of relationships, not ostracizing them.

It is through *permissiveness* that we reach healing and peace, not through even more draconian punishments and hurt inflicted upon people in the name of the nation or the name of 'worldwide democracy' and other slogans that veil the essential, the fact namely that it's political incompetence and large-scale ignorance of the functional logic of life

that got us at the point where we are today, facing worldwide ecological destruction, rampant crime, raising mental debility and emotional dysfunctions, raising child-neglect and youth suicide, depressions and a general nihilism that is actively fueled by the media because it makes for even higher profits.

In the current climate, the social, legal and political changes that I am proposing are certainly unpopular, but if they are not carried out, the situation will worsen to a point of no-return.

To give only one piece of information that stands for much more: there are now more than 800 prison camps in the United States, which are not ordinary prisons, but have been built in addition to ordinary prisons and jails.

They are camps, open-space areas that are carefully hidden from the public and that were built for hosting huge amounts of people, the biggest of them being able to hold approximately two million people.

Most Americans have no idea what's actually going on in their country, while the information is freely accessible on the Internet. Just do a Google

search under the keyword 'FEMA Camps.' Among the many contributions of highly concerned and outspoken citizens, you will also find 'debunking' information, which you can use to to find out how the system cunningly protects itself.

This is the reality we have to face, and without facing this reality, nobody can face his or her own inside, *emotional reality.*

If there is no waking up from the hypnosis of mass propaganda, I have written this guide for a future race to come. Be it so. I have written it for good use and in the hope that there will be a wake-up situation, individually and globally, before it's too late.

SOCIAL AND LEGAL POLICY CONSIDERATIONS

This chapter will show how *Emonics* can be useful in daily life; and this will then serve as a good example for showing that it's not just one more theory in a box of ivory tower knowledge, but a comprehensive scheme that will help understanding sexual attraction as a bioenergetic phenomenon.

It will help both the psychiatric profession and the concerned who actually are in the boat and who suffer from one or the other sadistic affliction or strange turn their sexuality has taken from a certain period in their life.

Let me first affirm that both professional help and selfhelp have to respect the individual's free will and therefore must therefore be optional. And if a person does not really suffer from their sexual sadism, then, by all means, nobody has the right to interfere in their life.

I say this very clearly here because voices to the contrary are being raised right now especially in the United States, Britain, Germany and France, and I have to remind the democratic setup of our constitutions that set the free will of the citizen as the first principle of our cherished democracies.

Even in case a criminal offense is committed, this does not give the state the right to force psychiatric treatment upon a person who does not wish to receive it.

Criminal law, as it is set and practiced since millennia, is a *retaliation system* of the state against so-called *offenders*.

Retaliation, revenge is all there is in this system! It is expensive beyond measure and brings as good as no educative or re-educative results. And it is perfectly ineffective from a point of view of legal policy!

Of course, it is another question to change criminal law by changing the underlying paradigm *from retaliation to cooperation*, and as a result to decriminalize all sexual behavior, as I have suggested this in a legal draft bill on unifying physical and sexual violence against children.

> —See Peter Fritz Walter, The 12 Angular Points of Social Justice and Peace: Social Policy for the 21st Century (2015).

Then, with applying a proactive paradigm of social interaction instead of retaliation, a system of *cooperative communication* with the citizen can be worked out, and entrusted expert consultants can help correct asocial and truly harmful behavior. After all, morality is not what a modern state reasonably

should focus upon; instead, the focus should be on preventing violence and abuse *through educating the citizen.* After all, it is only truly harmful behavior that can justify coercive state intervention.

The traditional system of sex laws and the persecution that results from them is truly a violation of both constitutional rights and fundamental human rights, whatever reigning authorities utter for justifying and whitewashing the abuses they commit almost daily through their unruly, insane and ignorant police forces, and their primitive, archaic and barbarous law enforcement institutions.

These reforms and precautions being taken to ensure the citizen is not coerced into treatment, I would make a number of suggestions for building *positive emotional identity* within the total realm of human sexuality. But let me first make sure that the notion of *emotional identity* is properly understood. It should be clear from the foregoing, but as this is important, I repeat it here once again. Emotional identity is identity, as a unique I-Am feeling, that is the result of an emotional predilection.

When Bernard F., the young educator that I used in my teaching tale, said he feels emotionally

attracted to children, this is an *emotional predilection*. Bernard, however, was not a pedophile, to repeat it.

> —The self-declared pedophile who goes public to defend the cause of pedophilia maintains a fake identity that puts sexual attraction to children as a hanger for lacking personal identity. The difference between a pedophile and Bernard is that the pedophile believes his sexual attraction defines him or her, as a person.

Bernard was not in the first place sexually attracted by children and maintained a long-term heterosexual relation with his girlfriend.

That Bernard got entangled sexually with some of the children is the result of his natural *pedoemotions* becoming sexualized, in one specific moment in time, in one specific situational context, with certain children and not with other children, and as a transitory kind of affair. This situation created a problem for Bernard, a problem at work and with the law, but this is not a reason to conclude Bernard is 'a pedophile.'

It is very important to grasp this, as the present legal system is not able to see this distinction because of its *ideological fixation*.

In other words, the sexualization of Bernard's emotional predilection for children in a specific time-bound situational context has to be considered as an *accident*, not as evidence for Bernard's assumed 'hidden' pedophilia. I know that this sounds like a justification but it's not. It is a scientifically and logically sound distinction that the present legal setup does not make, and wherefore it is, to say the least, incorrect, irrational, arbitrary, and dysfunctional.

Based on his emotional predilection for children, Bernard defined a large part of his identity, his professional choice, and also his choice for other than sexual love.

While Bernard maintained a sexual relation with an adult woman, he did not derive from this relationship the *emotional gratification* he needed and desired.

This is in no way a negative character trait of Bernard, but in the contrary what helped him achieve higher in life; it was the basis of his mission, so to

speak. His mission could be shortly described as caring for children who need care.

To conclude, if Bernard's emotional predilection for children is to be considered criminal, *then most of human behavior would have to be considered criminal* as what motivates us in life is what we feel emotionally strong for.

Then, the banker's emotional attraction for banking would be criminal, and a man who feels strong emotionally for Rolls-Royce cars would be criminal as well!

I know that at this point many readers will burst out in laughter, but there is really nothing to laugh about. What the present criminal law system does is *criminal* in that it punishes people for having emotional predilections, when only children are concerned.

As long as you feel emotionally strong for Rolls-Royce cars, all is fine in present society, but not so when you love children! Then you are a suspect, as by the very nature of your emotional setup. And this cannot be legal and constitutional, and therefore I am saying that sex laws are doing exactly what the

Church's Inquisition did a few centuries ago, only that it hurts many more people in our world because this criminal torture philosophy has gone global in the 21st century!

What the present book tries to convey is that in all sexual behavior, and in all sexual paraphilias, involved is *emotional identity as a condensation of emotional choice and predilection*, and this is something we have to respect, as it is ultimately human! It can never be made a legal offense within a democratic setup of society—provided this setup *really* is democratic—which I sincerely doubt!

What the present sex laws are doing implicitly is to condemn, persecute and punish emotional choice and predilection, and here is where they are transgressing the line to inhuman oppression and torture, as we know it from totalitarian forms of government.

I have chosen the case of Bernard as a mock trial that was inspired by many real court actions of a very similar character that I have found in the forensic literature.

HARNESSING THE POWER OF EMOTIONAL IDENTITY

Now, after this explanation, it may sound like a contradiction when, following up to my initial intent to give some guidelines for helping those who are concerned, I say this:

—Stay true to your emotional choice and predilection and do not waver! Do not stray from your intrinsic emotional vibration because if you do, you will end up in conformity and self-alienation and you will lose your unique creativity potential. Do not be afraid that one day your emotional choice may become sexualized; you don't need to be afraid because unlike Bernard, after having read this book and after having build emotional awareness, you will be shielded, able to handle whatever comes to you, and whatever endangers your safety. You will know how to handle the situation so as to ensure your safety and the safety of the children you care so much for!

And hereafter follow some precise suggestions you can use for this purpose, and that are inspired by the knowledge of the principles of *emotional flow*.

ALLOWING EMOTIONS

The first important thing is that you allow emotions, and especially those hot ones you hitherto repressed. Observe what happens when you do this! For example, you get in a violent rage and you allow it to happen, you do not fight it. You just passively watch and observe this rage, this hot energy moving, boiling in you.

What happens when you do this? You will observe that virtually within seconds *the emotion will change into another emotion*, as it is in the very nature of emotions to change in a kaleidoscopic manner when passive awareness is focused upon them.

Surprised? Indeed, most people when they experience this for the first time, are quite surprised, especially Westerners, as they are particularly alienated from their emotional life.

But that is not all. You will see that while the emotion has changed, there is something like a *driving force* that has not changed.

What is this driving force? It is your thought, your mental energy. In your mind, the roaming self-talk, the complaining, the hurtful accusations, the revengeful

ideas may still go on. When this happens, you may fall back into the rage time and again. This will teach you that it's actually your *thoughts* that control you, not your emotions!

This is what most people do not understand. They blame their emotions for their unruly life, their hassles in relationships, their bad fortune, not understanding the cause that triggers their emotional pattern. *It is thought, not emotional energy that is this cause.*

Your habitual thoughts mold your emotional pattern, so for changing this pattern, you have to change the way you think. When you harbor resentment against others, feelings of revenge, and violent thoughts in general, you bring a *disturbance* in your emotional pattern, and a *lasting disturbance* when you do this regularly. It means you get off your emotional balance, and then you go on and blame your emotions for all you have done to them by your unruly thoughts!

Once you understand that by *normalizing your thoughts,* you normalize your emotional energy, you are on the right track!

If you are not familiar with how to change your habitual thought pattern, and as a result your self-talk, try an old method that harnesses the power of your subconscious mind.

—See Peter Fritz Walter, Creative Prayer: The Miracle Road (Scholarly Articles, Vol. 5), 2015.

Do the work I am recommending, and you will see how as a result of changing your thoughts and your self-talk, you get your emotions back into a *state of natural harmony.*

Developing Emotional Awareness

Emosexual awareness is a term I coined for describing and teaching the specific awareness about our emonic (emotional) flow.

I have not taken them from any existing scientific or psychiatric treatise, as they are my own creation. Here are the definitions you may need to understand them.

EMONIC CURRENT OR EMONIC FLOW

The bioenergetic current flows through the organism, from the cell plasma to the periphery and into the luminous body and again back from the luminous body to the cell, depending on the polarity of the current. When it is positive, it is expansive and flows from the cell to the periphery (joy); when it is negative, it retreats from the periphery back into the cell (fear). Emonic flow, in popular language, may be expressed as *emotional flow*, and I do indeed use both terms synonymously.

These flow principles inherent in the nature of the bioenergy are also at work, negatively, in the etiology of sadism. In the natural sexual streaming of the bioenergy, that Wilhelm Reich described as 'hot, melting streaming,' the energy during orgasm explodes from the cell toward the luminous body. In sadism, however, because of the muscular armor in the pelvis region and other parts of the body, the energy cannot freely flow outwardly and therefore is repelled back with the result that instead of relaxing joy and expansive feelings, what is felt after orgasm is depression, anxiety, and fatigue. These latter symptoms then, can also be used as signals in diagnosing sadism. As a result of these insights, it is possible to actually heal sadism by getting the emonic current again to flow naturally through the entire organism.

This can be done through muscular *relaxation* or through consciousness work, using Life Authoring techniques, or else a combination of

these with methods practiced by alternative medicine, such as body work, massage, *Qigong*, *Tai Chi Chuan*, *Reiki*, or *Yoga*.

In the West, this kind of awareness was never popular while it was part of the *Hermetic Tradition;* in the East, body and energy awareness always was more developed, as it is part of any good meditation technique and thus also forms part of true religious teaching, both in Buddhism and Hinduism.

What is perhaps lesser known is that there are indices that Jesus of Nazareth was teaching this awareness as many other esoteric awareness techniques, but this knowledge was suppressed and traced out from the Bible by the Christian Church for obvious power reasons.

Today we are at a converging point of science and religion. My guess is that the scientific terminology will prevail over an esoteric and religious vocabulary because of obvious reasons of precision and clarity of expression.

This is why I have developed *Emonics* as a scientific vocabulary, not a religious teaching, but it is

well conceivable as such, and would not be a contradiction! Emotional awareness is a *specific awareness of your emotional and sexual attractions,* as volatile as they are when they come and go in your daily life, as they vary when you encounter various people, as they are fluid and not constant for the most part.

This specific awareness of your bioenergetic flow and its manifestation in the various emotions you experience is a gift that possesses a complete human, while it's absent in most of our highly fragmented contemporaries.

What does this awareness do? *Does* it do anything? Well, the amazing thing about any kind of awareness is that with humans, it's *reflective,* and that means it can be conscious of its own awareness. When you apply this now to your emotional flow, you will see that this awareness while it's passive, and apparently does not do anything, bears an effectiveness.

This is what it does without doing anything. It helps you observe, constantly monitor and control your emotions without actually controlling them.

This sounds paradoxical or illogic, but it's word for word true as it is written here.

The only sane way of controlling your emotions is *not* to control them, but passively watch them, by developing emotional awareness.

Krishnamurti would have said that you have to develop *total attention*, which means exactly what I am saying.

I do not hide that Krishnamurti's teaching helped me tremendously in developing my scientific ideas.

> —And I am certainly not the only one here; see only David Bohm's creative dialogue with K. over a number of years, partly reflected in the book 'The Ending of Time' that they co-authored. See, J. Krishnamurti, The Ending of Time, With Dr. David Bohm (1985). See also my own contribution to the understanding of K's teaching, Peter Fritz Walter, Krishnamurti and the Psychological Revolution, Great Minds Series, Vol. 1, 2015.

When you are aware of your emotional flow, and all the temporary or longer lasting emotional and sexual attractions you experience, they will never

overwhelm you, as it was the case with Bernard, the character from my teaching tale.

Then you are safe, without the need of policing yourself!

DEVELOPING SELF-VISION

The only thing that in the long run will channel your vital energies in constructive ways is *professional realization*, or working for a life's vision that you have set for yourself.

It means that you work on something for not just a few weeks or months, not even a few years, but for decades in a row, for such a broad vision will pull you forward on a constructive track.

This by itself, without working directly on the energy, can help the most virulently sexually active person to guard himself or herself from mishandling their sexual energy flow through abuse, dominance or sadism.

There are among geniuses many who would sit either lifelong in jail or in the madhouse, had they not instinctively followed this advice!

The sexual drive is strongest not among morons, clochards and sloths, but among our most highly developed souls, and among leaders, true artists and many spiritual gurus, and even saints.

The autobiographical literature is full of examples for this fact! And my own life experience is no different in this respect. I went through a major trial in my younger years for sexual misconduct with children that was fortunately cured through a psychotherapy I agreed to go through while in prison for three years. You may imagine that this major trial in my life of an educator was the primary motivational trigger for my research on emotions and sexuality, and for becoming a facilitator for helping people to cope with their sexual urges, and their temporary or lasting attraction to children, or else people in their care they feel sexually attracted to.

The advantage of directing your vision beyond yourself for a cause that goes beyond your little life is the energy transfer that comes with this dedication.

A great part of your virulent sexual energy that would disturb your peace of mind will then be channeled into constructive pathways, without you

really being aware of the whole of the process that this involves.

Behold, this does not mean that you become either impotent, or a saint!

But the urges will not plague you anymore, and you have your head free for conscious love choices that are somehow in alignment with the higher plan of your life, or superconsciousness.

Envisioning yourself means that you develop what other coaches call a *mission* for your life. I actually prefer *vision* over mission because the term vision metaphorically stands for 'seeing into the future.' I never saw anyone affirm that vision building helps channeling sexual energies, but it is so, in my own experience, and with *Emonics* it begins to make sense even for those who think it's a far-fetched idea.

Envisioning yourself doesn't mean that you focus exclusively on yourself. That would be the very contrary of it. It does mean that you envision yourself *as part of a higher order* that inscribes your work for the benefit of the whole of humankind, be this benefit of a scientific, artistic, commercial, or literary nature, be it to serve the progress of technology, lifestyle,

fashion, banking, politics or anything of interest for humanity.

It means that you feel powered from a fuel that is not entirely yours, but that somehow bears connections with cosmic energies that we know very little about. The very fact that you build and affirm this vision over and over, that you hold this vision over a longer time and thus bring constancy to it, makes it all happen by itself. For you will attract all the circumstances, people and resources conducive to the *realization of your vision.*

Becoming Flexible and Permissive

The most important ingredients in this new package I have for you and that is your selfhelp gift from this book are two characteristics or behavior modes that are among the most depreciated in patriarchal culture: it is *flexibility* and *permissiveness.*

Flexibility is a universal value that you see everywhere in nature. It is the moving and bending of young trees and the soft, pliable body of babies, and

the lesser moving and bending of old trees and elders.

Flexibility is directly related to the vital energy in that more vital energy means more flexibility, which implies being more pliable, and smooth; an absence of friction is also implied here. It's old trees that are broken by strong winds, because they are rigid and stiff, and their vital energies are reduced, while young trees that have a high vital energy potential are able to bend and thus can survive even a tornado.

Flexibility is also a value in direct connection with intelligence. I often use in my books the expression *flexible intelligence* when I talk about the East and Asian people, because it's one of their most visible characteristics.

Flexible intelligence helps the person to be adaptable, and to find satisfying solutions in situations that are not perfect in the sense that resources are lacking, as it's typically the case in lesser developed countries.

It means people are really inventive in finding ad-hoc solutions to virtually any problem, just by

using their little resources in an intelligent way, and thus *making the best out of nothing,* so to speak.

It also means to guard against rigidity in the insight that rigidity of mind leads to decay in effectiveness and also in relationships, while flexibility means to move with the energies not only of oneself, but also of others, and thus for example function well in a team.

In my genius research I have found flexible intelligence among geniuses being the most noteworthy character trait.

I have seen it in the lives of Leonardo da Vinci, Thomas Edison, Albert Einstein, Charlie Chapin, and Pablo Picasso, not because they are unique, but because I had a personal interest in their biographies.

It can be found in the lives of all geniuses, as genius is somehow a very flexible condition. It uses all available resources in the most economic way, thereby being highly functional and effective.

I found that all human genius is flexible and effective, which is why geniuses ultimately serve humanity; it's because what they do is not only useful but shows us our own potential genius, and here I

would add, it shows us that most of us other humans are *not flexibly intelligent enough!* Most people think that hard work will do and assure success but there is a dead end in every marathon.

Joseph Murphy writes in his book *The Miracle of Mind Dynamics (1964)* that hard work is not the answer to wealth and success. It's rather how you apply your mind to what comes in your way.

You can hit your head against the door; you can also open the door. And if there is no door, you can search for one, instead of running your head against the wall! The latter is what most people do when they encounter problems, ignorant about what Einstein coined in 'a problem cannot be solved on the same level of thought that created it.'

And this is actually a good example for what is flexible intelligence. It's a good way to express it, and let's not forget that Einstein dropped out of all schools and universities he was supposed to attend. It can't be different because our culture does the very contrary of teaching flexible intelligence, it teaches stubborn rigidity and dogmatic stupidity! That is the reason why Einstein and so many others of high

intelligence had to go their own way, including myself!

None of my books ever was accepted in traditional publishing, none of my music was ever accepted by a music publisher, none of my hundreds of drawings and art photos was ever triggering the interest of a commercial publisher.

Truly, my intention *is not commercial* in the first place, and such an intent needs its own channels.

Nobody but the theosophists published Krishnamurti's talks at first, and only in later years when he was already famous, his books were accepted in ordinary commercial publishing!

The other value that is highly depreciated, and even shunned in our culture is *permissiveness*. A culture so eternally judgmental and so hopelessly violent as American culture would be transformed *by the single value of permissiveness, without more!*

And by the same token, permissive education is today no more on the agenda of the values that this nation and most other Western countries foster, and I doubt it was ever before considered a value in the patriarchal cultural tradition.

The permissiveness I am talking about here is not directly related to education, while indirectly it has an impact on it. More precisely put, what I am talking about here is *self-permissiveness*, a form of latitude toward yourself, a tolerance toward yourself, especially when you are on your way of ascending in your evolution. The single most tiresome obstacle in this process is pressuring yourself, measuring yourself and comparing yourself to others. It really blocks your evolution. And this is the sad yet hidden reason why most selfhelp books actually are worthless; it's not because they are badly written but because they are applied in the wrong way.

They are sold, read and applied in a terribly competitive culture that says 'Well, now I know the way to go, and tomorrow I shall be different when I apply this new method.'

No, you shall not be different tomorrow, hopefully not! Or you have violated yourself. And that's not what you are supposed to do, for it will *not foster your evolution to coerce you into something, whatever it is.*

The author may not have intended that, but you yourself by applying his or her advice in a way that

shuns any self-permissiveness are virtually spoiling the soup by putting too much salt in it.

You are perfect as you are *now*. You shall be perfect tomorrow with a new inner composure. From your now to your tomorrow, there is a structural change to be made inside of you, in the whole of you, not just by turning on and off some switches or by reshuffling your character, or by accumulating some more knowledge about self-development.

This inner change, this structural transformation is a slow-moving process and that, if it is to endure, has to be deep enough to be effective. It has to penetrate into your subconscious mind and from there into your body, into every cell of your organism, so that it will be inscribed in your *vital energy code*, and signed into the intracellular information flow. It could be seen by a paranormal through a *change of colors in your aura*, for example.

To bring about such a change, which is true change, and not just the fake changes you see all around you every day and that are the shallow outcome of so-called 'selfhelp' as a global business, you need to be extremely flexible and permissive.

That does not mean to be sloth! It means to be consistent in your work on yourself, and it means to make one little effort at a time, one tiny step every day, but not a day without doing that tiny step.

You can see it and feel when you are permissive; there is an absence of strife, of pressure, of comparisons. There is a swinging within yourself, a feeling of unity, of harmony.

You are not counting the pages until the end of the book when you are permissive, for you know that it's not yet sunk deep into you, that you just got the overall information, and that the real work comes later; and that the real work means you open up for the *unknown to happen* and thus let the new go deeply inside of you, let it penetrate you without resisting it, without fighting it, without jubilating about your easy success.

No success is easy if it's to be a great success, for sure! Somebody once said that there is only *one* real obstacle to huge and lasting success. *It is small success.*

To summarize, by allowing your emotions, by developing emotional awareness, by developing

self-vision and by fostering flexibility and permissiveness on a daily basis, you are going to harness the power of your emotional identity. This is so because through these simple techniques, which are unknown to most people in our culture but are taught by all sages over all times, you will strengthen your emotional identity.

And what happens next?

Through strengthening your emotional identity you grow beyond your particular affliction, sadistic hangup or paraphilia.

Not that you will forget about it, not that you want a treatment against it, not at all, and much to the contrary. You will accept it to a point that you see the beauty of it because *your emotional identity has been affirmed.*

When your emotional identity is strong, you are not any longer separated from your love, but you *are* your love. Then, any strife that is inherent in the split between you and your loving attraction, between your identity and what you are doing and loving in life, has been healed, and then you are *one total unity.*

And then much good will flow from all your thoughts and your actions, without you being conscious of this good, for you have put aside all those false notions of good and bad that are part of the moralistic trash can.

When you apply emosexual awareness in your life, you learn to think and act *functionally*, economically, prudently, using all your resources in an effective way. Then, your particular way of loving and feeling erotic for certain people of your choice will not anymore be a problem as your inner split will be healed and you will become aware that where before you saw a problem with sex, there was actually a split in your consciousness.

And I have been explicit enough in this book to explain that this split also exists on the level of our culture, so the problem with sex is actually a cultural hangup, and not only your or my problem, on the individual level.

I have been explaining in other selfhelp guides that abuse is a cultural thing first of all, and that our culture actually conditions us to be abusive in that it denies us to really develop *autonomy* early in life.

—See Peter Fritz Walter, Power or
Depression: The Cultural Roots of Abuse
(Scholarly Articles, Vol. 6), 2015.

I have also explained that our culture virtually breeds *depression* by mass education that systematically disempowers and infantilizes children and adolescents, so that this cultural hangup actually represents *structural child abuse.* But we are not the victim of the culture that we were born in. We are not the clones of this culture, and we are not tin soldiers marching along to the slogans of this culture.

Many people are well like tin soldiers and their behavior patterns are not their own, because they are clones, not complete humans.

As such, they possess very little emotional awareness and are as a result often trapped by their passions.

You can go a different way!

BIBLIOGRAPHY

Contextual Bibliography

*

ARNTZ, WILLIAM & CHASSE, BETSY

What the Bleep Do We Know
20th Century Fox, 2005 (DVD)

Down The Rabbit Hole Quantum Edition
20th Century Fox, 2006 (3 DVD Set)

BERTALANFFY, LUDWIG VON

General Systems Theory
Foundations, Development, Applications
New York: George Brazilier Publishing, 1976

BORDEAUX-SZEKELY, EDMOND

Teaching of the Essenes from Enoch to the Dead
Sea Scrolls
Beekman Publishing, 1992

Gospel of the Essenes
The Unknown Books of the Essenes & Lost Scrolls of the Essene
Brotherhood

Beekman Publishing, 1988

Gospel of Peace of Jesus Christ
Beekman Publishing, 1994

Gospel of Peace, 2d Vol.
I B S International Publishers

BRENNAN, BARBARA ANN

Hands of Healing
A Guide to Healing Through the Human Energy Field
New York: Bantam, 1988

CAPRA, BERNT AMADEUS

Mindwalk
A Film for Passionate Thinkers
Based Upon Fritjof Capra's *The Turning Point*
New York: Triton Pictures, 1990

CAPRA, FRITJOF

The Turning Point
Science, Society And The Rising Culture
New York: Simon & Schuster, 1987
Original Author Copyright, 1982

The Tao of Physics
An Exploration of the Parallels Between Modern
Physics and Eastern Mysticism
New York: Shambhala Publications, 2000
(New Edition) Originally published in 1975

The Web of Life
A New Scientific Understanding of Living Systems
New York: Doubleday, 1997

The Hidden Connections
Integrating The Biological, Cognitive And Social
Dimensions Of Life Into A Science Of Sustainability
New York: Doubleday, 2002

Steering Business Toward Sustainability
New York: United Nations University Press, 1995

Uncommon Wisdom
Conversations with Remarkable People
New York: Bantam, 1989

The Science of Leonardo
Inside the Mind of the Great Genius of the Renaissance
New York: Anchor Books, 2008
New York: Bantam Doubleday, 2007 (First Publishing)

CHIA, MANTAK

Taoist Ways to Transform Stress into Vitality
Chi Self-Massage
Huntington: The Healing Tao Press, 1985

Awaken Healing Energy through the Tao
The Taoist Secret of Circulating Internal Power
New York: Aurora Press, 1983

CRAZE, RICHARD

Feng Shui
Feng Shui Book & Card Pack

London: Thorsons, 1997

EDEN, DONNA & FEINSTEIN, DAVID

Energy Medicine
New York: Tarcher/Putnam, 1998

The Energy Medicine Kit
Simple Effective Techniques to Help You Boost Your Vitality
Boulder, Co.: Sounds True Editions, 2004

The Promise of Energy Psychology
With David Feinstein and Gary Craig
Revolutionary Tools for Dramatic Personal Change
New York: Jeremy P. Tarcher/Penguin, 2005

EMOTO, MASARU

The Hidden Messages in Water
New York: Atria Books, 2004

The Secret Life of Water
New York: Atria Books, 2005

GERBER, RICHARD

A Practical Guide to Vibrational Medicine
Energy Healing and Spiritual Transformation
New York: Harper & Collins, 2001

HALL, MANLY P.

The Pineal Gland
The Eye of God
Kessinger Publishing Reprint

The Secret Teachings of All Ages
Reader's Edition
New York: Tarcher/Penguin, 2003
Originally published in 1928

GOSWAMI, AMIT

The Self-Aware Universe
How Consciousness Creates the Material World
New York: Tarcher/Putnam, 1995

HERRIGEL, EUGEN

Zen in the Art of Archery
New York: Vintage Books, 1999
Originally published in 1971

HUNT, VALERIE

Infinite Mind
Science of the Human Vibrations of Consciousness
Malibu, CA: Malibu Publishing, 2000

HUXLEY, ALDOUS

The Doors of Perception and Heaven and Hell
London: HarperCollins (Flamingo), 1994
(originally published in 1954)

The Perennial Philosophy
San Francisco: Harper & Row, 1970

KAPLEAU, ROSHI PHILIP

Three Pillars of Zen
Boston: Beacon Press, 1967

KARAGULLA, SHAFICA

The Chakras
Correlations between Medical Science and Clairvoyant Observation
With Dora van Gelder Kunz
Wheaton: Quest Books, 1989

KERNER, JUSTINUS

F.A. Mesmer aus Schwaben
Frankfurt/M, 1856

KIESEWETTER, CARL

Franz Anton Mesmer's Leben und Lehre
Leipzig, 1893

KINGSTON, KAREN

Creating Sacred Space With Feng Shui
New York: Broadway Books, 1997

KWOK, MAN-HO

The Feng Shui Kit
London: Piatkus, 1995

Lakhovsky, Georges

La Science et le Bonheur
Longévité et Immortalité par les Vibrations
Paris: Gauthier-Villars, 1930

Le Secret de la Vie
Paris: Gauthier-Villars, 1929

Secret of Life
New York: Kessinger Publishing, 2003
First published in 1929

L'étiologie du Cancer
Paris: Gauthier-Villars, 1929

L'Universion
Paris: Gauthier-Villars, 1927

Laszlo, Ervin

Science and the Akashic Field
An Integral Theory of Everything
Rochester: Inner Traditions, 2004

Quantum Shift to the Global Brain
How the New Scientific Reality Can Change Us and Our World
Rochester: Inner Traditions, 2008

Science and the Reenchantment of the Cosmos
The Rise of the Integral Vision of Reality
Rochester: Inner Traditions, 2006

The Akashic Experience
Science and the Cosmic Memory Field
Rochester: Inner Traditions, 2009

The Chaos Point
The World at the Crossroads
Newburyport, MA: Hampton Roads Publishing, 2006

LIEDLOFF, JEAN

Continuum Concept
In Search of Happiness Lost
New York: Perseus Books, 1986
First published in 1977

LONG, MAX FREEDOM

The Secret Science at Work
The Huna Method as a Way of Life
Marina del Rey: De Vorss Publications, 1995
Originally published in 1953

Growing Into Light
A Personal Guide to Practicing the Huna Method,
Marina del Rey: De Vorss Publications, 1955

MASTER LAM KAM CHUEN

The Way of Energy
Mastering the Chinese Art of Internal
Strength with Chi Kung Exercise
New York: Simon & Schuster (Fireside), 1991

MASTER LIANG, SHOU-YU & WU, WEN-CHING

Tai Chi Chuan
24 & 48 Postures With Martial Applications
Roslindale, Mass.: YMAA Publication Center, 1996

MCCAREY, WILLIAM A.

In Search of Healing
Whole-Body Healing Through the Mind-Body-Spirit Connection
New York: Berkley Publishing, 1996

MCTAGGART, LYNNE

The Field
The Quest for the Secret Force of the Universe
New York: Harper & Collins, 2002

MEADOWS, DONELLA H.

Thinking in Systems
A Primer
White River, VT: Chelsea Green Publishing, 2008

MYSS, CAROLINE

The Creation of Health
The Emotional, Psychological, and Spiritual Responses that
Promote Health and Healing
New York: Three Rivers Press, 1998

NAU, ERIKA

Self-Awareness Through Huna
Virginia Beach: Donning, 1981

NI, HUA-CHING

I Ching

The Book of Changes and the Unchanging Truth
2nd edition
Santa Barbara: Seven Star Communications, 1999

Esoteric Tao The Ching
The Shrine of the Eternal Breath of Tao
Santa Monica: College of Tao and Traditional
Chinese Healing, 1992

The Complete Works of Lao Tzu
Tao The Ching & Hua Hu Ching
Translation and Elucidation by Hua-Ching Ni
Santa Monica: Seven Star Communications, 1995

NI, MAOSHING

The Tao of Nutrition
3rd Edition
With Cathy McNease
Los Angeles: Tao of Wellness, 2012

ONG, HEAN-TATT

Amazing Scientific Basis of Feng Shui
Kuala Lumpur: Eastern Dragon Press, 1997

PONDER, CATHERINE

The Healing Secrets of the Ages
Marine del Rey: DeVorss, 1985

REID, DANIEL P.

The Tao of Health, Sex & Longevity
A Modern Practical Guide to the Ancient Way
New York: Simon & Schuster, 1989

Guarding the Three Treasures
The Chinese Way of Health
New York: Simon & Schuster, 1993

SANTOPIETRO, NANCY

Feng Shui, Harmony by Design
How to Create a Beautiful and Harmonious Home
New York: Putnam-Berkeley, 1996

SCHULTES, RICHARD EVANS, ET AL.

Plants of the Gods
Their Sacred, Healing, and Hallucinogenic Powers
New York: Healing Arts Press
2nd edition, 2002

SHELDRAKE, RUPERT

A New Science of Life
The Hypothesis of Morphic Resonance
Rochester: Park Street Press, 1995

SIMONTON, O. CARL ET AL.

Getting Well Again
Los Angeles: Tarcher, 1978

STIENE, BRONWEN & FRANS

The Reiki Sourcebook
New York: O Books, 2003

The Japanese Art of Reiki
A Practical Guide to Self-Healing
New York: O Books, 2005

TALBOT, MICHAEL

The Holographic Universe
New York: HarperCollins, 1992

TANSLEY, DAVID V.

Chakras, Rays and Radionics
London: Daniel Company Ltd., 1984

TATAR, MARIA M.

Spellbound: Studies on Mesmerism and Literature
Princeton, N.Y., 1978

TILLER, WILLIAM A.

Conscious Acts of Creation
The Emergence of a New Physics
Associated Producers, 2004 (DVD)

Psychoenergetic Science
New York: Pavior, 2007

Conscious Acts of Creation
New York: Pavior, 2001

TOO, LILLIAN

Feng Shui
Kuala Lumpur: Konsep Books, 1994

WALKER, N.W.

The Natural Way to Vibrant Health
Prescott, AZ: Norwalk Press, 1972

WATSON, GEORGE

Nutrition and Your Mind
The Psychochemical Response
New York: Harper & Row, 1972

WATTS, ALAN W.

The Way of Zen
New York: Vintage Books, 1999

This Is It
And Other Essays on Zen and Spiritual Experience
New York: Vintage, 1973

WYDRA, NANCILEE

Feng Shui
The Book of Cures
Lincolnwood: Contemporary Books, 1996

Yang, Jwing-Ming

Qigong, The Secret of Youth
Da Mo's Muscle/Tendon Changing and Marrow/Brain Washing Classics
Boston, Mass.: YMAA Publication Center, 2000

The Root of Chinese Qigong
Secrets for Health, Longevity, & Enlightenment
Roslindale, MA: YMAA Publication Center, 1997

Young, Robert O.

The pH Miracle
Balance Your Diet, Reclaim Your Health
With Shelley Redford Young
New York: Grand Central Life & Style, 2010

PERSONAL NOTES

www.ingramcontent.com/pod-product-compliance
Lightning Source LLC
Chambersburg PA
CBHW030419290526
45786CB00001B/45